on track ...
Ultravox

every album, every song

Brian J. Robb

sonicbondpublishing.com

Sonicbond Publishing Limited
www.sonicbondpublishing.co.uk
Email: info@sonicbondpublishing.co.uk

First Published in the United Kingdom 2024
First Published in the United States 2024

British Library Cataloguing in Publication Data:
A Catalogue record for this book is available from the British Library

Typeset in ITC Garamond Std & ITC Avant Garde Gothic
Printed and bound in England

Graphic design and typesetting: Full Moon Media

Follow us on social media:
Twitter: https://twitter.com/SonicbondP
Instagram: www.instagram.com/sonicbondpublishing_/
Facebook: www.facebook.com/SonicbondPublishing/

Linktree QR code:

on track ...
Ultravox
every album, every song

Brian J. Robb

sonicbondpublishing.com

Special thanks

Special thanks to Rob Kirby of the *re:VOX* fanzine and Stu Entwistle of Ultravox Unofficial on Facebook (and across social media) for their much-appreciated editorial feedback. Any errors or omissions remaining are purely those of the author, as are all opinions expressed.

on track ...
Ultravox

Contents

Introduction 9
Ultravox! (1977) 14
Ha!-Ha!-Ha! (1977)..22
Systems Of Romance (1978) 30
Vienna (1980)...38
Rage In Eden (1981)..51
Quartet (1982)..62
Lament (1984)...74
U-Vox (1986) 86
Revelation (1993)..97
Ingenuity (1994) 105
Brilliant (2012)...111
Bibliography 119

Introduction

If there's one track most music fans know by Ultravox, it's their popular 1981 hit single 'Vienna', and the fact that this iconic track was kept from the top spot in the UK thanks to an irritating novelty song by Joe Dolce titled 'Shaddap You Face'! With four weeks stuck at number two, 'Vienna' nonetheless became the sixth best-selling single of that year. Losing the top spot was an egregious injustice in British musical history, one the often-too-serious band never lived down. However, it may have also done them a favour, as Ultravox made an indelible mark on 1980s pop music despite never reaching number one – their only other top-five single was the zeitgeist-capturing 'Dancing With Tears In My Eyes', which reached three in May 1984. Between 1981's 'Vienna' and 1984's 'Love's Great Adventure', Ultravox scored 12 top-30 hits (17 reached the top 40) and seven top-ten albums.

Though their final album (to date) was 2012's *Brilliant*, Ultravox have existed in one form or another for the better part of five decades. With their 1980s frontman Midge Ure still enjoying a hugely successful solo career (he's the hardest-working man in showbiz, seemingly always touring, either solo or with a band), the band's DNA continues to prosper.

Founded by their original vocalist John Foxx (born Dennis Leigh in 1948) in April 1974, the band – then named Tiger Lily – arrived during the punk years (a musical style some of their early songs toyed with, notably 'ROckWrok', 'Fear In The Western World' and 'Young Savage'). They were more interested in the post-punk new wave that swept through music after 1976. Their art-rock poise saw them signed to Island Records, the band now operating under the name Ultravox! (complete with exclamation mark), issuing the trio of late-1970s albums *Ultravox!*, *Ha!-Ha!-Ha!* and *Systems Of Romance*. These albums were diverse, exploring the clash between Foxx's cold machine-like songs and keyboard player Billy Currie's classical training and instrumentation. Despite their best efforts and significant support from their live show audiences, early Ultravox! albums and singles failed to reach any UK charts.

Their music evolved with the standard guitar-and-drums approach, supplemented first by Currie's distinctive electric violin, an early Roland Rhythm 77 drum machine and a saxophone on the prototype synth-pop of 'Hiroshima Mon Amour', the final track on *Ha!-Ha!-Ha!*. Despite their innovations, the band were largely met with indifference by the music press, as *Sounds* (19 August 1978) noted: 'Ultravox! exist in a media limbo. Although they constantly attract big audiences, the general media view seems to be that they are, quite frankly, pretentious'.

The first of several reinventions came in 1978 when they not only dropped that tricky exclamation mark but replaced guitarist Stevie Shears with Robin Simon. *Systems Of Romance* – the third and final album from this initial version of Ultravox – developed their sound further, thanks to a collaboration with German producer Conny Plank, who'd worked with krautrock outfits like Neu! (who the early Ultravox! had lifted their exclamation mark from) and Kraftwerk. The evolving sound saw a greater use of synthesizers combined with traditional rock instruments and Currie's classical approach. Several of the *Systems Of Romance* tracks – including 'Slow Motion', 'Quiet Men' and 'Dislocation' – pointed to the band's 1980s evolution. Despite the evident innovation at play, *Systems Of Romance* had no commercial impact (even with positive critical coverage in the often-sniffy music press), and Island decided to cut their losses, finally dropping the band. This saw an increasingly frustrated John Foxx embark on what became a successful solo career, with his first album *Metamatic* in 1980.

In the wake of the seeming dissolution of Ultravox, Billy Currie took up an offer to tour and record with synth-pop pioneer Gary Numan (an avowed Ultravox fan) in 1979, Canadian drummer Warren Cann went to work with New Zealander Zaine Griff, and bass guitarist Chris Cross played shows with James Honeyman-Scott (of The Pretenders) and Barrie Masters (from Eddie and the Hot Rods). Guitarist Robin Simon had remained in the US at the end of Ultravox's early-1979 tour. It seemed the band had come to a premature end.

Currie found himself involved with a new project – the studio-only band Visage included among its members the 26-year-old Midge Ure. Ure was an experienced musician who'd already enjoyed a degree of chart success and fame in the 1970s with proto-boy band Slik and also played with the Rich Kids (with Visage drummer Rusty Egan) and Thin Lizzy as a guitarist and later keyboard player. Egan encouraged Currie to recruit Ure to front a new iteration of Ultravox. Ure recalled in Dylan Jones' history of the New Romantics *Sweet Dreams* (2020): 'Towards the end of 1979, I was asked to join Ultravox. There was no plan; I kind of fell into it. When I joined Ultravox, I wanted to be part of a rock band. I wanted it to be something experimental; I wanted it to be art rock ... I was allowed to kind of experiment and play and be led by these three other guys who had much more experience in that world than I had'. While Currie and Cann had reservations about bringing in an experienced *pop* musician (Ure wrote songs, sang, and played guitar and keyboards), bassist Chris Cross was all in favour of the development – as he told *Electronic Sound #69* in 2020: 'I distinctly remember not being flavour of the month, because I was arguing that it sounded like a good idea. Where Midge was coming from was completely different. It was like with the original version of Ultravox, only this was even more different. I knew we were perfectly capable of doing the experimental stuff, but I thought the idea of having someone more tune-based was interesting. I didn't know if it would work or not, but it all fell into place after that'.

Ure had no particular mission in mind to *save* Ultravox. He simply saw becoming a member of a band – whose earlier work he'd admired – as a positive next step for him. Ure admitted to *Electronic Sound*:

The three guys I was joining knew a lot more about the technology and the whole electronic creative process than I did. I wasn't going in there to fix something or to make something better; I was going in to make the noise I'd heard in 'Slow Motion' and 'Quiet Men'. That sound was so exciting, and I was going to be a part of that ... It wasn't about aiming for success; it was about being a part of something that was so far removed from Slik that it was like being on another planet – and musically, it probably was. Bear in mind that this was three years after Slik had been to number one with 'Forever And Ever'. All of a sudden, I'm in this synthesizer art-school rock band, not worrying about trying to write three-minute pop songs but thinking about what we could create without any parameters. That was the driving force, and it completely overshadowed any thoughts about upsetting the odd John Foxx fan.

The new 1979 Ultravox fusion laid the foundation for their dramatic (in contrast to the John Foxx years) 1980s chart success. New songs came quickly, and the band were able to issue the new album *Vienna* (on Chrysalis Records) in July 1980. The first single, 'Passing Strangers', saw them finally crack the UK singles chart (only at 57, but it was a start). The second single 'Sleepwalk' reached 29 – the band breaking into the top 30 for the first time – while *Vienna* peaked at number three in the UK album chart. All this was a level of success Currie, Cann, and Cross had not experienced previously, putting to rest any doubts they initially had about teaming with Ure. Things got even better with the 1981 single release of the title track 'Vienna', which stayed at number two in the UK for four weeks, gaining infamy evermore for being kept from the top spot by John Lennon and then Australia-based Joe Dolce.

The 1980s were hugely successful for the retooled Ultravox. Each album cracked the UK top ten – *Rage In Eden* (four), *Quartet* (six), *Lament* (eight), and even the fan-derided *U-Vox* at number ten. The band became one of the most successful acts of the era, capped by their 1985 appearance at the Live Aid concert, partly due to Ure's involvement with Bob Geldof in the Band Aid project that put the Ure/Geldof co-write 'Do They Know It's Christmas?' at number one in the UK for five weeks across Christmas 1984 and into the new year. In some ways, it was Band Aid/Live Aid that sowed the seeds of the end of the most successful incarnation of Ultravox. Pursuing a solo career, Ure scored a number-one hit in his own right with 1985's 'If I Was', while his debut solo album *The Gift* reached number two in the UK. Regrouping, Ultravox produced their final album of the 1980s – the controversial *U-Vox* – without drummer Warren Cann. Tensions between Ure and Currie were making life increasingly difficult, and the new musical directions evident in the *U-Vox* material didn't find favour with many fans. The October 1984 non-album single 'Love's Great Adventure' (promoting the 1984 greatest hits package *The Collection,* which reached number two in the UK) was Ultravox's final UK top-30 hit, peaking at number 12. In the wake of the commercially successful yet critically derided *U-Vox*, the band went their separate ways – Ure to a solo career, Currie to producing his own instrumental albums, Cann to pursue a possible acting career in L.A. and Cross to retrain in psychology.

The 1979-1986 version of Ultravox was distinctive, cultivating a collective image in support of the music. Austere black-and-white band photos adorned the stark cover of the *Vienna* album, while the title track's music video broke new ground. Ultravox became known for their iconographic videos, which were often mini films that told a story across three or four minutes ('Passing Strangers', 'Vienna', 'The Thin Wall', 'The Voice', 'Reap The Wild Wind', 'Hymn' and more). Director Russell Mulcahy guided the band through the first few videos, but from 'The Voice' through to 'Love's Great Adventure', Midge Ure and Chris Cross were behind the image the band collectively projected.

Inevitably, the 1980s Ultravox were tagged as New Romantics despite their music, videos and image being very distinct from the likes of Duran Duran or Spandau Ballet. Perhaps it was this failure to fit into a clearly-defined New Romantic niche that caused the music press to often keep Ultravox at some distance – they were never embraced in the way some other 1980s bands were, despite turning out hit after hit. As a live band, Ultravox surprisingly proved themselves to be a formidable rock outfit that used not only synthesizers but classical instruments when it suited the music. Each album was supported by significant tours across Europe.

Ultravox also stood out by pioneering the use of clear vinyl for their singles. They'd discovered that – unlike black vinyl – clear vinyl was produced from non-recycled elements, leading (or so the band believed) to a sharper sound. Working with producers like Conny Plank (*Vienna*, *Rage In Eden*) and George Martin (*Quartet*) prepared the band for self-producing their later albums *Lament* and *U-Vox*. They also included instrumentals, opening *Vienna* with the seven-minute epic 'Astradyne' and working extended instrumental sections into *Rage In Eden*. It was the 'Vienna' single that typified their unconventional musical approaches, which they maintained across their chart-reaching output through the decade, constantly changing and evolving (sometimes in directions their fans didn't entirely appreciate). It was a degree of success that was difficult to recapture beyond the 1980s.

After that classic hit-making lineup split in 1986, Billy Currie attempted to revive Ultravox without the participation of any other previous members, releasing two albums featuring two different lead singers (1993's *Revelation* with Tony Fenelle, and 1994's *Ingenuity*, with Sam Blue, co-produced by Currie), but little notice was taken by either fans or the music press, and the project was abandoned by 1996. It wasn't until the 30th anniversary of *Vienna* that a proper reunion of the 1980s lineup took place, resulting in the 2009 *Return to Eden* UK tour and the 2010 *Return To Eden II* tour of Europe. While recording wasn't the band's intention during the live reunion tours, thoughts soon turned to producing new music, resulting in 2012's *Brilliant* album.

The band's final live performances came in April 2013, supporting fellow 1980s stars Simple Minds for four UK dates. By 2017, Currie – always keen to keep Ultravox alive – finally came to the conclusion that the band had run its course after over 40 years. That same year, Midge Ure spoke to the *Daily Express*: 'I think it's probably finished. It was lovely to come back five years ago and do those shows. It was great to make up again, not that we really fell out, but we'd moved our separate ways. After 20-25 years of heading in different directions, to come back and perform those songs one more time, it was a glorious thing to do'. Ure – the band's youngest member – celebrated his 70th birthday with a concert at London's Royal Albert Hall in October 2023. While he's still creating new music, repackaging old classics and continuing to tour, chances are the band will never perform or record together again, especially following the death of bassist Chris Cross in March 2024, aged 71. Whatever happens, the classic songs remain, as Ure pointed out: 'These songs are old enough that they've been part of people's lives for most of their lives. And [the fans are] very precious about those things, just as I am.'

In 2020, Midge Ure summed up the Ultravox legacy to *Electronic Sound*: 'Ultravox were all about creativity, we were about trying to make something interesting. It wasn't for everybody, but then nothing is. You want to be perceived as something unique, and Ultravox were certainly that.'

Ultravox! (1977)

Personnel:
John Foxx: lead vocals, acoustic guitar ('I Want To Be A Machine'), harmonica
('Saturday Night In The City Of The Dead')
Stevie Shears: guitars
Warren Cann: drums, backing vocals
Chris Cross: bass, backing vocals
Billy Currie: keyboards, violin
Producers: Brian Eno, Ultravox!, Steve Lillywhite
Recorded at Island Studios, Hammersmith, London, autumn 1976
Label: Island
Release date: 25 February 1977 (UK)
Charts: UK: -, US: 189 (Cashbox), SWE: 25
Running time: 38:04

In the early 1980s, many young fans of the popular Midge Ure incarnation
of Ultravox may have been surprised to discover the existence of the earlier
John Foxx-led group. Those who became teenagers in 1980 were just too
young to have experienced punk as active record buyers, so the 1976-1979
Ultravox! and the trio of albums they produced passed those listeners by
and remained an unknown quantity. They'd have been even more perplexed
to discover that the roots of their favourite band reached as far back as
1973/1974: the height of the prog rock era.

The initial founder of the band was Royal College of Art student Dennis
Leigh, who later styled himself as 'John Foxx'. Leigh once declared, 'John
Foxx is more intelligent than I am, better looking, better lit.'. Leigh's glam-
rock outfit operated under the name Tiger Lily (taken from J. M. Barrie's
1904 play *Peter Pan*) and consisted of Foxx on vocals, Chris St. John (born
Christopher Allen, later known as Chris Cross) on bass, and Stevie Shears on
guitar. Chris Cross recalled in *Classic Pop*'s 2020 *SynthPop Special Volume
II*: 'Art, film and music were starting to interweave more. The timing was
perfect. Dennis was the catalyst and a great instigator'. They formed in
London in April 1974 but realised they needed a drummer. In Jonas Warstad's
in-depth online interview with Warren Cann on the earliest days of Ultravox!,
the British-Canadian Cann recalled simply responding to a 'drummer wanted'
ad in *Melody Maker*. 'I just turned up at the audition', Cann told *ZigZag* in
1984. 'As soon as we rehearsed together, I realised we had something quite
special'. Cann liked the sound of Foxx's songs, so he signed up in May 1974.
'The idea was to be the London Velvets', said Foxx in *Sweet Dreams* – Dylan
Jones' history of the New Romantic movement. 'We even had a base in a
factory at King's Cross!'.

At this point, the band had not played any gigs and were simply developing
their material in rehearsal at the Royal College of Art (Foxx and Cross were
still students there). In August 1974, the four-piece Tiger Lily made their

live debut in Chorley, Lancashire – Foxx's home town. According to Cann, Foxx used his connections to arrange a gig in 'a local youth club's hall'. This served as a warm-up for what they considered their true debut gig: London's Marquee Club, supporting Heavy Metal Kids, at the end of August. Before the end of 1974, the band added a fifth member: classically trained violinist William (known as Billy) Currie.

Drawing heavily on glam acts like David Bowie, Roxy Music and New York Dolls, Foxx set out to mix his songwriting and performance approach with classic 1960s pop groups like The Beatles and The Rolling Stones (bands he was to turn against later in the decade: see 'Life At Rainbow's End'). Tiger Lily only released one single – a cover of Fats Waller's 'Ain't Misbehavin' through Gull Records on 14 March 1975, with an original B-side titled 'Monkey Jive'. Through their next few gigs, the band cycled through several monikers, including The Damned ('...for a week or two until we discovered another band had beaten us to it' (Warren Cann)), The Zips, London Soundtrack and Fire of London. By October 1976, they'd settled on Ultravox!. According to Foxx in *New Musical Express* on 13 July 1977: 'It sounds like an electrical device, and that's what we are'. Many of the songs composed during the Tiger Lily years were to appear on their debut album *Ultravox!*.

'Looking back now, it was an exciting time', recalled Cross. 'Something was changing'. *Ultravox!* scored a handful of reviews. In *Record Mirror* on 12 March 1977 under the witty headline 'Voxy Music', Seamus Potter noted: 'The wide range of ideas far surpasses any piracy of musical styles ... Roxy Music and Bowie, consolidated by Eno's production, have both made their indirect contribution, but a band with so much to offer are unlikely to need any musical crutches for long'. In *NME* on 23 April 1977, Phil McNeil commented:

> Energy and anger have little to do with the romantically bored pose Ultravox! strike ... Shears and Currie, and even Foxx, are sublimated to the mood at all times, and the underlying mood of the record is coldness ... (Foxx) writes a good tune, mind. Every song is memorable, and only 'Lonely Hunter' is boring, and that's saved by the intricate yet simple machinery riffs. They really do carry off the machine sound well.

McNeil concluded that while he didn't like Ultravox!, he liked their album.

'Saturday Night In The City Of The Dead' (Foxx) 2:35

A fairly straightforward rock 'n' roll track opens the album; more Cockney Rebel than Roxy Music. Ultravox! were clear that their earliest work was reflective of their lives in London (perhaps about London's 'home of punk', the Roxy), and so it is with this song (sometimes styled as 'Sat'day'). They no doubt spotted the 'all night boys in the Piccadilly Arcade', had seen the 'Tottenham Court Road litter, skitter in the wind', and they'd spent their time 'in the dole queue, face like a statue'.

There's something proto-rap in Foxx's rapid-fire rhymes ('Spiked hair, don't care, Oxfam outlaw'), but the track was created right on the cusp of punk. That's evident in the live performance captured on the EP *Live At The Rainbow* (recorded in 1977, released in 2022), where Foxx all but leaps off the stage. However, his pub-rock harmonica bits cut into the track's punk cred. There's a rawness to this opener that's rarely recaptured on the rest of the tracks (only 'ROckWrok' from *Ha!-Ha!-Ha!* comes close), but it does suggest an equally valid direction in which the early Ultravox! could've moved. Seamus Potter's *Record Mirror* review described the track as 'a misleading opener ... for all its crashing rock 'n' roll energy, it doesn't serve as an intro to yet another new wave ensemble'. The song is inherently simple – about the teen longing for the freedom of Saturday night on the town, where 'The city's pretty dead but I'm still alive'. The collective enterprise that was Ultravox! – driven by Foxx's art-student interests – felt they had so much more to offer.

'Life At Rainbow's End (For All The Tax Exiles On Main Street)' (Foxx) 3:44

Guitars and drums are to the fore in this ripped-from-real-life story. Foxx is 'The cold boy from the suburbs' who moves to the big city in search of fame and fortune. The concept of 'Life At Rainbow's End' is the good life – fortune and security – achieved in a deal with the Devil. Having had 'a good introduction from a formerly trusted friend', the singer achieves the good life he sought, having made the necessary sacrifice and having 'burnt all the maps that lead here' he's denied anyone else the opportunity of following. There's a price to pay – his lofty isolation leads to 'lonely parties' and 'the dark side of this world'. It's a reading validated by its deconstructive destructive climax where the instrumentation collapses into cacophony. This was seen as Foxx's riposte to those 1960s bands who'd made it big and then either split or indulged themselves (mainly The Beatles and The Rolling Stones; the title recalls the Stones' 1972 album *Exile On Main St.*). Having 'made theirs', they were seen by the up-and-coming proto-punk 1970s generation as having pulled up the ladder to success behind them. However elegiac and sceptical the song might be about the possibilities of fame and fortune (the pot of gold at the end of the rainbow; the quiet life on easy street) through rock 'n' roll, it's a much stronger pointer to the future of Ultravox! (and certainly to the hit-achieving Midge Ure era). That was the view of Seamus Potter in *Record Mirror*: '(It establishes) the overall mood, firmly – Billy Currie's swirling violin offsets the intense, anguished vocals of John Foxx with occasional harshness'. In *NME*, Phil McNeil noted Foxx's inspirations – 'Foxx puts-on his Bryan Ferry voice for 'Life At Rainbow's End', as Brian Eno gets his clanky production into stride; rhythm section mixed high and thuddy, a very non-hero guitar sound for Stevie Shears, who's always plinking towards the periphery with attractive grey tones, and a wide range of colourless tones from keyboards/ violin player Billy Currie'.

'Slip Away' (Currie, Foxx) 4:19

The first true Ultravox! epic 'Slip Away' is three songs in one. As the first track with a writing contribution from a band member other than Foxx, the extended instrumental second half has Billy Currie's nimble fingers all over it. Lyrically, it's a word salad in search of meaning. There are hidden gems buried here: 'All things blow by me/My sorrows have sails'. Overall, the lyric simply exists to accompany the music. Verging on prog (though not quite as long as the next track), it starts as a pop song, but the pretension is strong. The first section is engaging enough, driven by drumming and piano flourishes over which Foxx's voice sails (whatever the lyrics mean). The 'Just wasting time section' suggests an entirely different track before it goes off in yet another different direction with the lengthy instrumental epic that follows Foxx's fade-out line 'dissolve'. This is Currie strutting his stuff uninhibited, and it's delightful. It doesn't connect with the earlier material, and it's very much of the mid-1970s (punk-prog, perhaps), but it is great pretentious fun. The final barely audible tingle sends 'Slip Away' off into the night.

'I Want To Be A Machine' (Currie, Foxx) 7:21

This was one of their earliest songs (then under the Tiger Lily moniker), was possibly the first song Foxx wrote, and had been part of their live set for a while alongside 'Life At Rainbow's End', 'Dangerous Rhythm' and 'Lonely Hunter'. These songs were on a demo tape that secured their initial deal with Island Records, but as a last-minute check, they were summoned to play live in a conference room at Island's Hammersmith HQ. If the latter half of 'Slip Away' turned that track into an epic, Ultravox! were only just beginning.

Unlike the sometimes-frantic pace of the album's earlier songs, 'I Want To Be A Machine' opens with a more-stately approach, the initial fairy-tale lyric backed by acoustic guitar. Each chorus adds instrumentation, becoming more insistent and – in the electric guitar and drums – machine-like. Currie's violin begins in-earnest after the second chorus, connecting to the final verse. It dominates the final run, faster than before, driven by drums, through to Foxx's conclusive cry of 'Ah!'.

Perhaps inspired by Fritz Lang's 1927 film *Metropolis* ('In mitternacht, die mensch-maschine'), the lyric features many *modern* obsessions of both popular versions of Ultravox – 'cathode face', 'video souls', 'flesh of ash and silent movies', 'broadcast me' and 'In the star cold beyond all of your dreams'. The song's subject was to influence many Foxx songs: 'I was looking at the next stage of evolution, as we merged ourselves with new technologies. What would it feel like? ... (I saw) the need for a new combination of genre and ideas, a kind of romantically despairing sleaze mixed with sci-fi'.

An effective closer to side one, this saw Foxx zoom in on an obsession that would provide him with material for years to come. Oddly, he sings 'nebula' as 'nee-bula'!

'Wide Boys' (Foxx) 3:16

Written around the time the band signed with Island, 'Wide Boys' was another ripped-from-real-life song: 'Our environment and lifestyle was our subject matter,' said Warren Cann of their earliest inspirations. 'Almost everything on the first album is about what it was like to be living in London at that time'. Perhaps the band thought of themselves as wide boys, defined as a 'British slang term for a man who lives by his wits, wheeling and dealing'. 'Wide' in this context means 'wide awake' or 'sharp-witted'.

This is the closest Ultravox! ever came to a teen anthem: 'With the wide boys/Up on the streets/Wide boys/Ah, go on and meet me/Wide boys/Delightfully unpleasant'. Some have seen the entire inspiration for Duran Duran's oeuvre in this track.

'Dangerous Rhythm' (Cann, Cross, Currie, Foxx, Shears) 4:16

The first single (released on 4 February 1977) has been dubbed the white reggae track. Its creation was laid at the door of Shears' taste for reggae and the influence of fellow Island artists. *Record Mirror* dubbed it 'cosmic reggae', noting the 'heavier-than-lead bass and ice-cold vocals', calling the result 'very weird and wonderful'. In *NME,* it was called 'by far their most memorable number, a reggae abstraction, mesmeric, simple, and subliminal, with Ferried vocals'.

The demo had been recorded by Steve Lillywhite at the old Phonogram Studios near Marble Arch, where (according to Cann) Lillywhite had been engineering for the likes of Status Quo and Rolf Harris. Through Lillywhite, Ultravox! had access to the studio in downtime. 'We experimented a lot and did our best to learn how to use it all', recalled Cann. The band were to return to Phonogram for their second album. As a debut single, 'Dangerous Rhythm' was an interesting enough choice to capture attention (as the reviews show) but gentle enough not to be too challenging (as much of the album was).

For Seamus Potter in *Record Mirror*: "Dangerous Rhythm' hypnotises throughout. It's off-beat and easily justifies its choice for single release'. *Sounds* liked it too: 'Their youth bestows upon them a direct brashness ... rich emetic bass, precise Ringo drums, synthesizer cascades, and Eno's hand in the production make this a most confident debut single'.

Brian Eno's production credit came to annoy Cann: 'We produced the record, gave Steve Lillywhite and Brian Eno credit as co-producers, and all they ever say is 'produced by Eno'. It makes me angry because it is no more accurate than it is true. He only worked on three or four songs at the most ... to be fair, his name did help bring about some attention that might not otherwise have been paid to us concerning that first album. The record company had a *name* involved with the record, so that's what they pushed in order to boost interest and sales'.

Unfortunately, 'Dangerous Rhythm' didn't bother the singles charts.

'The Lonely Hunter' (Foxx) 3:42

Another life-on-the-streets song from Foxx, this one sees him move from his cod-Bryan Ferry approach and begin to develop a more distinctive vocal style. Perhaps the weakest track on the album, it's certainly the most straightforward. The 'lonely hunter' appears to be a teen on the prowl for romance, though the lyric has some atmospheric film-noir echoes, like the downtrodden private detective in pursuit of his prey: 'My collar's up and my coat is sleek'. The noir connection was to be developed even further in terms of image *and* music in the Midge Ure era. As it is, the track is short and inconsequential.

'The Wild, The Beautiful And The Damned' (Cross, Currie, Foxx) 5:50

This 'gloriously grandiose' (*Classic Pop*) track first appeared in October 1976 on the Island Records *Front Runners* compilation oddly titled *Rock & Reggae & Derek & Clive*. Cann recalled: 'The record contained a track each from Island's artists and was available as a special-offer sampler in conjunction with *Melody Maker*, for 65 pence'. The other artists included Robert Palmer, Bunny Wailer, Max Romeo and Burning Spear, alongside Peter Cook and Dudley Moore, explaining their names in the title. Here, the band weren't billed as Tiger Lily or Ultravox! but simply as '?', as they'd yet to settle on a name. Cann said, 'We knew that whatever we told them (Island) would be the name we would be branded with forever, and we wanted to be sure we were happy with our choice. They had to get the record out and couldn't wait for us to make up our minds, hence the '?' for us beside 'The Wild, The Beautiful And The Damned''. Cann also explained the unusual method Ultravox! was then using to develop their songs:

> We'd write a song, try to perfect it, then move on to another song; then we'd go back and dissect the previous song and either make it better or salvage its best elements and proceed to incorporate them into the newer song, leaving the shell behind. It was a great experience in the art craft of songwriting ... 'The Wild, The Beautiful And The Damned' came together after a week or two of constant experimenting with its essential elements. But once we felt we had it, that was basically it, and it never changed after that. We felt that the song represented at the time – as much as any one song could – what we were all about. We always knew it would be (included) when it came time to record an album.

From the violin opening, it's instantly something different and the album's defining track. It's catchy, musically impressive (Currie lets loose) and lyrically baffling: perfect Ultravox!. Why it wasn't the single, we'll never know. Foxx had ambitions beyond music, poetry being one of them. His collection of short stories and poems titled *The Quiet Man* was four decades in the making and was finally published in 2020. It's clear the lyrics of this song are as much abstract poetry as any attempt to construct a narrative. Fantastic images abound: 'Calling cards of madness', 'the stunted and the dreamless ones', 'the latest venereal journals', 'catalogs [sic] of fear', all located in Berlin alleyways under the auspices of the New York fuhrer! The song stops for a brilliant couplet: 'Break my legs politely/I'll spit my gold teeth out at you'. What does it all mean? The lyric has a ready answer: 'Don't ask for explanations/There's nothing left you'd understand'.

'My Sex' (Cross, Currie, Foxx) 3:01

As well as closing the album, 'My Sex' was the B-side of the 'Dangerous Rhythm' single. Synths are finally to the fore on this Eno-produced track, which samples a Phil Collins drum rhythm from Eno's track 'Sky Saw' from his third album *Another Green World* (1975). Bits of 'Sky Saw' also turn up in Eno's *Music For Films* (1978).

Throughout his early songwriting, Foxx drew on the literature of British new wave sci-fi writer J. G. Ballard – particularly his short story collection *The Atrocity Exhibition* (1970) and the novel *Crash* (1973). Foxx described Ballard as 'the first radical and relevant novelist of this technological age'.

Attempting to describe the abstract feelings involved in sex in concrete terms, Foxx draws on Ballard imagery directly: 'My sex/Is invested in/ Suburban photographs/Skyscraper shadows on a car crash overpass'. He even manages to work in the title of Ballard's 1975 novel *High-Rise*: 'My sex/Is an image lost in faded films/A neon outline/On a high-rise overspill'. Quoted in the 2005 *Q* magazine *Electro-Pop Special Edition*, Foxx admitted: 'I was very interested in the push-and-pull of romanticism and alienation. It's the opposite of punk's anger. There's something very romantic about withholding certain feelings. 'My Sex' was the first electro-ballad. When we finished that, I knew it was a direction no one else was anywhere near at that point'.

The description of Ballard's themes in *The Oxford Dictionary Of National Biography* (2013) is easily applicable to Ultravox!: 'a preoccupation with Eros, Thanatos, mass media and emergent technologies'. Songs of sex and death permeate the Ultravox! catalogue, while themes of mass media (film, television, radio) abound. The phrase 'emergent technologies' proves to be as much a medium for the band to realise their groundbreaking sound as it is a theme.

Related Tracks
'Ain't Misbehavin' (Brooks, Razaf, Waller) 3:10

The 1929 jazz song 'Ain't Misbehavin' was featured in the 1943 movie *Stormy Weather*, played by pianist 'Fats' Waller. It had featured in a variety of Broadway stage musicals, becoming a standard, and was a favourite of jazz trumpeter Louis Armstrong, who noted, 'It was one of those songs you could cut loose and swing with'.

The Ultravox! version was commissioned for an unnamed film about 'blues greats and vintage porn', according to Warren Cann. The band took the 'several hundred' pounds they were paid and invested in an electric piano for Billy Currie, 'so he wouldn't have to stand around ... when he wasn't playing the violin'. Foxx and Tiger Lily's take on the song is very different to the original, with Foxx unmistakably applying Brian Ferry-style singing. It's a languorous take, heavily featuring Currie's distinctive violin.

As a single, Tiger Lily's 'Ain't Misbehavin' vanished without a trace, not resurfacing until the 2000 compilation *Glitterbest: 20 Pre Punk 'N' Glam Terrace Stompers*. The single cover (designed by Martin Patton, an eventual co-founder of the Some Bizzare label) showed the band posing around the head and shoulders of a female shop mannequin, taken in the band's rehearsal space, which was also occupied by a mannequin refurbishment business.

'Monkey Jive' (Leigh/'Foxx') 3:35

Perhaps the 'Ain't Misbehavin' B-side is of more interest. The opening crunching rhythm immediately identifies it as Foxx-era Ultravox!, though he takes more of a Hawkwind/Robert Calvert vocal approach, with echoes of Sparks in the music. There are also echoes of Roxy Music, especially their third single 'Street Life' from *Stranded* (1973). The echo of 'Street Life' in the similar speed of vocal delivery obscures the lyric, though the opening line 'I'm tired of hanging around street corners' also echoes 'Street Life'.

Essentially the first Ultravox! track, 'Monkey Jive' is significant, even if it contains little that might be identified with the later versions of the band. Nonetheless, there's enough here to suggest that – as Foxx no-doubt fervently believed – there was to be a future in the sound beyond being merely a Roxy Music knockoff.

The producer of both sides of the single was graphic artist and filmmaker (*Rainbow Bridge*, 1972) Austin John Marshall (who died in 2013 aged 76), who worked on the English folk-revival scene with his wife Shirley Collins (they divorced in 1970). Gull reissued the single in 1977 as Ultravox!, as did Martin Patton's Dead Good Records in 1980, with the song sides flipped. It saw further release in France in 1981.

Ha!-Ha!-Ha! (1977)

Personnel:
John Foxx: lead vocals, guitar ('Hiroshima Mon Amour')
Warren Cann: drums, vocals, rhythm machine ('Hiroshima Mon Amour')
Billy Currie: viola, keyboards, synthesizers
Chris Cross: bass, vocals
Stevie Shears: guitar
C. C. Mundi (Gloria Mundi): saxophone ('Hiroshima Mon Amour')
Producers: Ultravox!, Steve Lillywhite
Recorded at Island/Phonogram Studios, Hammersmith, May-June 1977
Label: Island
Release date: 14 October 1977 (UK)
Charts: -
Running time: 34:40

Thanks to youthful energy and driving ambition, Ultravox! released a
second album in 1977. Their music shifted from glam-rock and Roxy
Music influences, moving into the two seemingly contradictory directions
(suggesting a war of musical styles at the heart of the project) of punk and
electronic.

Still backed by Island, who maintained their faith despite their debut's
lack of impact, there was enough funding to significantly upgrade the
band's equipment. Increasing their use of synthesizers, they invested in an
ARP Odyssey and a Roland TR-77 drum machine, both of which made their
presence felt on *Ha!-Ha!-Ha!*'s closing track 'Hiroshima Mon Amour'. Foxx
explained in *Sweet Dreams*: 'The point of using synthesisers was to find out
what these strange new instruments could do that hadn't been done before'.
The new technology became central to the music's creation, but it was
troublesome, according to Warren Cann:

Chris had bought our very first synth: an EMS Synthi. It was a strange
contraption contained in a briefcase, with the keyboard being a flat plate on
the inside of the lid! It was weird and wonderful but highly temperamental
and very unstable. It had to warm up for about an hour, and even then,
it would never hold its tuning. About all it was ever used for was sound
effects, which didn't require being in tune.

Cann made specific signature use of the Roland TR-77, which only came
with presets and was not programmable: 'What we loved about it was the
mesmerising effect of the absolutely constant *perfect* rhythm and tempo.
It never faltered, it just continued to hypnotically pump out the rhythm.
It fascinated me'. Billy Currie also updated his electric violin and electric
piano, which came with a set of useful pre-programmed string settings
(making it a kind of synth). For the 2006 sleeve notes of *Ha!-Ha!-Ha!*, Foxx

commented: 'Bill was classically trained, but hadn't let this kill his originality or aggression. He was out to make synthesizers compete with the power of guitars. He went flat-out to destroy and succeeded'.

There's a maturity to the lyrics throughout this album (mostly from Foxx), with the band largely moving away from the commentary on teenage life that dominated *Ultravox!*. Instead, alongside the widening musical and rhythmical palette, the subjects expanded in focus.

Pursuing his own projects, Brian Eno opted out of *Ha!-Ha!-Ha!*, leaving the band and Steve Lillywhite to handle production. The result was a heavier sound, befitting the punk ethos of the time, thick with harsh feedback and aggressive instrumentation. Foxx later told *Q* magazine: 'We were trying to increase base frequencies for the synths, subsonic zooms – we wanted to work like sonic terrorists, to make audiences sick'. The result was often a difficult listen that gave no quarter to the audience, with tracks switching between rampant punk thrash ('ROckWrok') and electronic ('Hiroshima Mon Amour'). It's as if the songs themselves were fighting for dominance, for the right to define the band's future sonic direction.

Reviewing *Ha!-Ha!-Ha!* for *Sounds* on 22 October 1977, Pete Silverton claimed Ultravox! had 'mostly rejected the possibilities of the accessible pop song, using only catchphrase choruses (often with infuriating insistence), and relied wholesale on what they probably see as the avant-garde, and the more-cynical soul might feel were mere noises'. He noted the record's 'unrelenting seriousness ... humanity is the last thing you'll find in Ultravox!', branding the songs as 'an uneven mixture of the adventurous, the orthodox (especially the arthritic drumming) and the wilfully different', complaining that the band were the result of 'the bad effects the mere acquisition of a synthesiser can have'.

In *NME* on 15 October 1977, 18-year-old Julie Burchill complained that the band (in their 20s and – in Foxx's case – 30s) were old. 'There are weary hints at masturbation and eyeliner (sigh) – you're still doing things I gave up admitting to years ago. I'm an ice machine, but you're not because you brag about it too much. The real machine always does the best impersonation of a human being ... I may be cold, but thank God I ain't old'.

Given that by this time, punk was in its second wave, it seemed clear that any follow-up would have to move in a fresh direction. Post-punk verging on art rock could only take Ultravox! so far. It was time to embrace new wave.

'ROckWrok' (Foxx) 3:34

The album's only single (out on 7 October 1977) opens with a loud, fast sound focusing on sex. Somehow the lines 'Come on, let's tangle in the dark/Fuck like a dog, bite like a shark' escaped the attention of the often-censorious BBC Radio-1 DJs, possibly due to Foxx's speedy delivery. Cann admitted, 'We were very excited to hear this played on the BBC, not only because it was one of our songs, but because they apparently hadn't noticed the naughty lyric'.

There are interesting lyrics throughout, with the title itself a stand-in for sexual intercourse. There's 'Penetration boys in hotel lifts' and 'An anal sailor in the bar, bar', while 'The chaste and the chasers, amazing the neighbours' are 'Gay, wild and willing, stripped of grace'. Ultimately, 'Austerity makes you want to ROckWrok'. From the opening clicking rhythm through the screaming catchy chorus to the sneaky false ending and the final title vocal sign-off, the opening track is a table-setting barnstormer.

Though Foxx liked to style himself as the Marcel Duchamp of pop, it seems the unusual title styling was not inspired by Duchamp's surrealist publication *Rongwrong* (a sole issue published in May 1917), but according to Cann, 'It was spelt that way simply because that's how John Foxx wrote out the song information for the sleeve. He wanted it spelt in that particular fashion. I can only presume he thought it looked better that way'. Cann also admitted to an unusual and traditional musical inspiration for this most punk-sounding track – he'd lifted the rhythm from Chubby Checker's 'Let's Twist Again', which gives this very-1970s track a kind of early-1960s throwback feel.

The single didn't trouble the charts, though it was taken note of much later – Massive Attack played the song on their 2019 tour (having previously sampled it on 'Inertia Creeps'). It also turned up on the soundtrack of cult TV series *Sex Education* (season one, episode eight, 2019) in a scene where the characters Lily and Otis attempt to conquer their sexual fears, putting the John Foxx-era Ultravox! in the musical company of The Cure and Sigue Sigue Sputnik.

The single B-side was an 'alternate version' of album closer 'Hiroshima Mon Amour'.

'The Frozen Ones' (Foxx) 4:07

This was released as a single in West Germany only, where it failed to make an impact. The deceptively quiet opening with finger-clicks soon bursts into punk life, if not as fast as 'ROckWrok'.

There are interesting lyric concepts, some more relevant to the early 21st century than they ever were to 1977. The line 'Too many pictures on my screen, all of them screaming at me' suggests nothing less than contemporary social media, reinforced by the following lines: 'Thought I had this insulation/ The only way to stop the flood, whenever feelings get too real/Is to cut the information'. A 21st-century interpretation might see this as Foxx suggesting abstinence from mobile phone use and social media before such things even existed.

The song builds to an extended ending, with the title repeated until it fades. According to Cann:

> The ending fade on this song reflected something we'd often do – when recording the backing track, after having repeated the chorus a few times of a song, we knew we'd fade out; we'd begin to just let rip until we were

going crazy, and not stop in the studio until either one of us made a colossal mistake or we got tired or fell about laughing. Or all three. Sometimes, the greatest bits of the song were unusable because they'd occurred two minutes after the song had ended.

The German B-side was an alternate version of 'The Man Who Dies Every Day'.

'Fear In The Western World' (Cann, Cross, Currie, Foxx, Shears) 4:00
Driven by Shears' throbbing guitar, this punk outcry comments on the late-1970s news cycle. Engaging with the idea of a 'media myth' forming the truth of things for the population's 'TV orphans', the lyric engages with the headlines of the day: 'Ireland screams/Africa burns/Suburbia stumbles/The tides are turned'. The lyric plays out over frantic drumming and slightly queasy violin sounds. Foxx continued to push boundaries with his lyrics (as on 'ROckWrok') with couplets like 'Someone told me Jesus was the Devil's lover/While we masturbated on a magazine cover', guaranteeing the track an absolute ban on radio play. 'The audience finds itself on the stage' was likely inspired by Andy Warhol's 1968 comment that in the future, everyone will be famous for 15 minutes.

In a tumble of confusing sounds and feedback, the track crumbles to a definitive end. The noisy exit was 'almost an entity unto itself', according to Cann:

We had about five minutes of [feedback] and came close to giving it a title and putting it on the album as-is. Why didn't we? As much fun and anarchic as that would've been, we realised that much of the public might not think so after a few listens (we thought it got better with each listen), and mainly we thought it too self-indulgent of us to take up a whole song's space on an album with such an extreme piece – unlike the critics, whom we were only too happy to piss off. Still, it was always extended live to the pain threshold and beyond!

'Distant Smile' (Currie, Foxx) 5:21
The prior track cuts to this piano intro, which Cann described as being like 'tumbling through chaos into a lake of serenity'. It doesn't last as it morphs into another fast rocker. Foxx indulges in some extravagant vocal exercises accompanying the piano notes before the guitar bursts into life alongside the insistent drums. It continues until a breakdown, with the instruments battling for dominance. Though it's as punk-oriented as the previous tracks, Foxx stretches his vocal approach more with some recall of the Ferry/Eno influences that pervaded their debut album.

It's a fitting closer for side one, wrapping up the album's driven punk sound, and is a clearing of the decks, allowing side two to branch off in a more experimental vein that would lay the groundwork for the third and final Foxx Ultravox album *Systems Of Romance.*

'The Man Who Dies Every Day' (Cann, Cross, Currie, Foxx, Shears) 4:10

A distinct change of pace and style opens side two. While there's plenty of guitar up front, the synthesizer line dominates. Foxx's rhythmic delivery of the obscure lyric drives the song forward, while Currie lets loose with a synth solo. The Ultravox (now *sans* exclamation mark) that would come to be is created here, preparing to burst free from its chrysalis – a marching rhythm, staccato bass and synthesizer sounds combined with lyric allusions to mystery ('A silhouette, a cigarette, and a gesture of disdain'), magic ('You always play that funny pack of cards without an Ace'), cinema and even the distinct film-noir genre ('You flicker like a shadow, moving like a thief') would proliferate from here, while songs about mystery men would multiply. According to Cann:

> Bill's synth was being incorporated into the sound more and more. This is one of the songs that really pointed to where we wanted to go in the future, and we knew it. The bass line is interesting in that it could so obviously be a synth-bass line. It has all the hallmarks of one, yet it was still being played on bass guitar.

'Artificial Life' (Currie, Foxx) 4:59

The new sound continues here with a more punky overlay, even if the lyric recalls the teen nightlife that dominated the previous album. Across a packed five minutes, 'Artificial Life' captures the exuberance of late-1970s clubland, especially the brand new styles of the Blitz club established in 1978, from which the New Romantic scene would emerge, including Midge Ure's Ultravox. In *We Can Be Heroes: London Clubland 1976-1984* (2011), writer Graham Smith chronicled a period he'd experienced firsthand. Though the Foxx incarnation of Ultravox! slightly pre-dated the establishment of Blitz, the subculture that would be associated with that venue emerged from a variety of club nights that ran through the mid-1970s. The lifestyle celebrated and condemned in 'Artificial Life' was already happening when the song was written. Chronicling the exploits of 'refugees from suburbia', Foxx charts the competition to impress youthful club-goers, whether through dress (which would become central to the Blitz) or dancing. The chorus hints at the joy and deathlessness of the experience that 'goes on all night, all night/And it goes on and on, the artificial life'. There's nothing real about this alternative universe created across the weekends by those fleeing the mundane, everyday late-1970s life. However, things turn bleak as the 'game' begins to fall apart – 'Blunked on booze', one character 'ran through divine light, chemicals, Warhol, Scientology, her own sex/Before she turned away'.

Foxx captures the desperate search for new sensations and stimuli. The scene collapses into a 'whirlpool' that has such 'seductive furniture': 'It's so pleasant getting drowned/So we drink and sink and talk and talk/With interchangeable enemies and friends'.

Currie's synth is drowned out by the more traditional crunchy guitar-and-drums combo that comes to the fore, but he also all-but-destroys a violin in the process of capturing 'Artificial Life', given the strangulated sounds as the track breaks down.

'While I'm Still Alive' (Foxx) 3:16

The morning after, it's another celebration of youth, when time means nothing and there's all to play for: 'Strutting my stuff/I'm blagging the damage' and 'The fighting's exciting/The age is dramatic'. Compared to the previous two tracks, it's all a bit basic, and Foxx falls back on his Ferry impersonation, crossed with a little of The Sex Pistols' John Lydon. The most interesting moment is at the end – a last gasp of the punk that Ultravox! had played with on *Ha!-Ha!-Ha!*, that's rather out of place amid all the progressive tracks that make up side two. Cann agreed: 'While not without its charms, this is probably the weakest song on the album, and to my mind, represented the last of where we'd been. How apt that it's followed by 'Hiroshima Mon Amour', which represented where we were going'.

'Hiroshima Mon Amour' (Cann, Currie, Foxx) 5:13

Taking its title from the 1959 Alain Resnais movie, which boasted a non-linear storyline, this track is widely agreed to be the early Ultravox! masterpiece. According to Cann, though placed last on the album, it was the first track recorded. Cann talked to Jonas Warstad:

> We'd previously done a demo, a rockier type of arrangement, but it presented an ideal opportunity to try out the drum machine, so it was rearranged for the TR-77. We were in Phonogram studios, and C. C. – a sax-playing friend of Bill – was invited down to blow over the track to see what would happen. Normally, we never wanted anything on our records that we hadn't actually played ourselves, but this time, we were prepared to make an exception if it sounded good. The backing track was played to C. C. a few times in the control room for him to listen to and then he went into the studio and did two takes. We chose the first take.

The change in sound is apparent immediately. The Cann-hacked drum machine starts with a hypnotising rhythm, compounded by the drone of a synth and an unusual saxophone blast, building to Foxx's opening line: 'Somehow we drifted off too far.' The quintessential example of Euro *art pop* that would become an Ultravox speciality going forward, 'Hiroshima Mon Amour' draws on the past to point to the future. Everyone is in top form, and the ghostly saxophone only adds to the melancholy, bringing heartfelt emotion to the cold drum-machine sounds. Yes, there are allusions to the dropping of the atomic bomb ('Future's fused like shattered glass/The sun's so low/Turns our silhouettes to gold'), but that's not the subject. Memory ('Walk through Polaroids of the past') and the ending of relationships ('Communicate like distant stars/Splintered voices down the phone') play through the lyric.

The earlier demo B-side is much more abrasive, with a more lively vocal, a central discordant instrumental break and no saxophone. It's the electro album cut that's definitive. Kraftwerk fused with Roxy Music and The Velvet Underground gave birth to something very different: a future new-wave direction for electronically driven music. Foxx declared, "Hiroshima Mon Amour' focused everything I was trying to get to at that point'.

Related Tracks
'Young Savage' (Cann, Cross, Currie, Foxx, Shears) 2:56
A lost Ultravox! classic? Paired with 'ROckWrok', 'Young Savage' proudly displays the punk roots from which the more sophisticated Ultravox would ultimately emerge. It also provides a thematic accompaniment to 'While I'm Still Alive' and several debut album tracks that celebrate the exploits of youth. When not being obscure or abstruse, Foxx proved himself to be an able chronicler of mid-1970s youth subcultures (not bad, considering he was about 30 at the time). At the same time, the song captures the despair that lurks behind the smiles and the dancing: 'Live too fast for love or sorrow/ Look behind the face, it's hollow'. He tells of the 'stranger', the 'subway dweller', the type who populated the clubs 'taking bites from every kiss', with 'coloured hair, cheap tattoos'. In fact, as with 'While I'm Still Alive', Foxx appears to anticipate the surface concerns of the Blitz scene before it even emerged – 'Every sneer is thrown away/With practised gestures of disdain/ The outlaw stance is so pedantic/Hate the world, it's so romantic'. Perhaps his age – which disassociated him from the 20-somethings in the clubs – does show after all. As it is, the clever and interesting lines are buried under an undoubtedly catchy post-punk throb and rhythm that powers along. *Sounds* dubbed it a 'cocaine-brain speed cocktail', while *NME* said it had 'dire semi-melody, terrible chorus line and spotty-sounding words'.

'Modern Love' (Cann, Cross, Currie, Foxx, Shears) 2:31
This live recording from London's Rainbow Theatre was the A-side of the free single issued with the first 10,000 copies of *Ha!-Ha!-Ha!*. 'While we liked it, we'd never have put it on an album, so it was chosen to go on the free single', explained Cann. Guitar and drums are much to the fore on this simple would-be pop song. However, there are some interesting phrases buried in the vocal, like 'Vampire gangsters with miles of smiles and reams of dreams' and 'All I need is a chemical vacation/I'll take a video stroll through the life

exchange'. Even on relatively minor material, Foxx was lyrically unable to stop drawing on Ballardian imagery and cinematic tropes.

'Quirks' (Cann, Cross, Currie, Foxx, Shears) 1:40

Ultravox! do The Sex Pistols filtered through 1950s pop on this short throwaway that was the B-side to the free *Ha!-Ha!-Ha!* single. Cann claimed, "Quirks' was a song we'd written which was, as they say, short and sweet. We were very fond of it. We weren't particularly inclined to deliberately lengthen a song if its duration had suggested itself naturally, so we left it alone. It was a natural for a B-side'.

Systems Of Romance (1978)

Personnel:
John Foxx: lead vocals
Warren Cann: drums, vocals, rhythm machine
Billy Currie: keyboards, violin
Chris Cross: bass, synthesizer, vocals
Robin Simon: guitars, vocals
Producers: Conny Plank, Ultravox, Dave Hutchins
Recorded at Conny Plank's Studio, Cologne, West Germany
Label: Island
Release date: 8 September 1978 (UK)
Charts: -
Running time: 36:09

There were two major changes to Ultravox! in 1978. First, the Neu!-emulating exclamation mark was dropped. Cann recalled, 'After *Ultravox!* and *Ha!-Ha!-Ha!*, we'd had rather enough of exclamation marks. Besides, while fun in the beginning, it was becoming more hassle to keep it than lose it, so we just dropped it'. Also dropped was guitarist Stevie Shears. There's confusion over whether he left of his own volition, was fired, or it was mutual. Towards the end of recording *Ha!-Ha!-Ha!*, the band started exploring their musical direction. Their *Retro* EP (released on 10 February 1978) consisted of live versions of 'The Man Who Dies Every Day' and 'My Sex' (from a Huddersfield Polytechnic gig), 'The Wild, The Beautiful And The Damned' (from the Rainbow Theatre gig – released more-fully in 2022 as *Live At The Rainbow 1977*) and 'Young Savage' (from a The Marque, which Cann said was 'my all-time-favourite live recording of ours, and perfectly captures the energy of those Marquee gigs'). The *Retro* EP (on 7" single; the Australian 12" including 'Quirks' and 'Modern Love') cleared the decks, musically speaking. *NME* tagged the live performance as offering 'some hints of futurism here, a threat of cybernetics there, a hint of asexuality, a suggestion of languid decadence, a whiff of narcotics, a *je-ne-sais-quois* of French for that certain chicness'.

Cann recalled: 'By the time we'd mostly finished touring for *Ha!-Ha!-Ha!* and began casting our thoughts towards the next album, we knew it was time for changes to be made. While a loyal and dependable bandmate, Shears' guitar playing had for some time become an increasingly limiting factor in how we arranged the songs, and it appeared that the only solution was a parting of ways'. Whatever went down, Shears' departure was abrupt. He participated in several subsequent musical ventures, including Faith Global and Cowboys International.

Shears was replaced by Robin (formerly Robert) Simon, seemingly brought in by Billy Currie, who knew him from the Halifax music scene and his participation in the London-based band Neo in 1975/1976, who'd supported Ultravox! several times at the Marquee. Cann noted:

While younger than us and relatively inexperienced, Robin Simon was invited to join, and the difference was invigorating. He had an accomplished and fluid style, which I think is immediately apparent on our first recorded work with him, *Systems Of Romance*. As I recall, he had ten days to learn our songs and then immediately found himself in Holland with us doing a tour – in at the deep end.

Simon brought the use of guitar multi-effect pedals and an amplifier with tremolo to the band, resulting in a more multi-dimensional sound. He also joined Currie's experiments in feeding synthesizer sounds through guitar effect pedals to create new and unique sounds.

The band felt they were on the brink of something big. They'd used up all their pre-Island material and had worked off their remaining punk aggression recording *Ha!-Ha!-Ha!*. They were now ready to create something unique, a sound they could claim as belonging uniquely to them. Foxx focused on a science-fiction what-if question: 'What if America had never existed? What would Brit music sound like if we'd looked to Europe instead? I felt exultant when I reached the point of asking myself that, and I suddenly knew what we had to invent'. That led to a total change of scene for the recording of what became the third album *Systems Of Romance*. The band had fallen out of love with London and the teenage nightlife they'd so often emulated in their songs. The new recording environment chosen – the studio of producer Conny Plank near Cologne in West Germany – gave rise to a new sound.

Konrad 'Conny' Plank – a fixture on the so-called krautrock scene of the 1970s – had worked with bands that heavily influenced the early Ultravox!, notably Neu! and Kraftwerk. As an electronic music pioneer, Plank focused as much on soundscapes (whether natural and shaped by electronics or entirely artificial) as he did on rhythm and melody. In 1977, he'd worked with Brian Eno and, as a result, recruited Dave Hutchins from Island as an engineer and mixer. It was Plank, as much as the experimentation and ambition of Foxx and company, that brought a new edge to Ultravox – one that would survive through the two best albums of the Midge Ure era: *Vienna* and *Rage In Eden*.

Reviewing *Systems Of Romance* in *NME* on 9 September 1978, Ian Penman wrote: 'Occasionally – as on 'Slow Motion' – Ultravox produce a pretty electronic pop song ... even this is negated however, by dint of Eno-esque lyrical diarrhoea ... This is weedy, idealistic, pessimistic verbiage which utilises the appealing angles and ignores the aggravating ones'.

In *Record Mirror*, Philip Hall dubbed Ultravox 'the forgotten band of the new wave. Hopefully, this album will change all that. It confirms their position as one of the more imaginative and forward-thinking bands of the moment ... Ultravox experiment but never become self-indulgent. The clever use of keyboards enhances rather than drowns the compact songs, which always remain sharp ... 'Quiet Men' is a pounding anthem, while final track 'Just For A Moment' is a shimmering piece of haunting romance'.

'Slow Motion' (Cann, Cross, Currie, Foxx, Simon) 3:29

Right from the opener 'Slow Motion', *Systems Of Romance* presents itself as very different to the two preceding albums. Robin Simon's guitar sound is immediately apparent, blending successfully with Currie's synthesizer lines, complimenting the more conventional bass sounds throughout. Of the new sound, Cann noted, 'It perfectly represented our amalgamation of rock and synthesizer, many of the aspirations we had gelled in that song'.

Where 'Hiroshima Mon Amour' had left off in recording the difficulties of communication, 'Slow Motion' picked up and carried the ideas forward. The swooping synth opening is a marker of the future, while the rhythmic thumping and insistent drumming were a sound rarely heard elsewhere in 1978. The epic sweep of Foxx's vocals is offset against Currie's violin stabs and wall-of-sound synth effects. Simon's guitar work shreds away between choruses, slashing through what amounts to an overall epic sound. According to Cann, 'Slow Motion' was 'one of those songs where everything seems to fit together perfectly to form an entity greater than the sum of its parts'. 'Slow Motion' was also one of three Foxx-era songs that Midge Ure performed with Ultravox at a gig in St Albans in August 1980 (along with 'Quiet Men' and 'Hiroshima Mon Amour').

The single was released in August 1978 ahead of the album but failed to crack the UK top 100. Despite that, 'Slow Motion' remains a quintessential Ultravox track and the sound of the future arriving early.

'I Can't Stay Long' (Cann, Cross, Currie, Foxx, Simon) 4:16

This is another appearance of Foxx's mystery-man figure – later defined as the quiet man – that preoccupied him. Observation from a distance – as if by an alien – is the viewpoint in this and several other Foxx songs at the time (and beyond). The figure describes experiencing the time and tide of the seasons as if they were unfamiliar as if he'd come from another place. He's a visitor ('Because I, I can't stay long') who can 'drift through all the walls/ And let the scenery dissolve'. The language of images and cinema feature: 'dissolve', 'flicker', 'roll on'.

Initially, the shimmering synths sound like a continuation of 'Slow Motion', but it soon moves to more of a rock vibe, albeit against substantial synth melodies throughout, colliding and coalescing with the vocals, leading to an extended instrumental outro. The song manages even without a traditional chorus, unusually, while exhibiting a structure that hooks the listener. Certainly, one listener who might've been hooked was Gary Numan. Much of his earliest work with Tubeway Army suggests he'd paid attention to Ultravox: specifically, 'Slow Motion' and 'I Can't Stay Long'.

'Someone Else's Clothes' (Currie, Foxx) 4:25

Questions of identity continue, driven by a strong guitar riff. A muddy middle section gives pause while the synths hijack the track, suggesting an entirely different and much darker song. The exuberant vocal and guitar riffs have a more poppy approach than Ultravox had attempted before, but they couldn't help but drift off in contradictory directions as if their instruments weren't happy with mere pop. Again, an extended instrumental finale ends the track, but even *that* feels like it comes from an entirely different track.

A Frankenstein of a song, 'Someone Else's Clothes' sounds as the title suggests: like a bunch of borrowed, mismatched items slung together through necessity rather than choice. It's as though Foxx and Currie were pulling in different directions, and neither could dominate. The band have moved on from their early infatuation with Roxy Music, instead seemingly emulating The Cars or even the novelty output of someone like Lene Lovich (her 'Lucky Number' was recorded as a B-side for her cover of 'I Think We're Alone Now' in July 1978, but re-released in 1979 as an A-side, reaching three in the UK). All in all, 'Someone Else's Clothes' feels like a leftover from an earlier album.

'Blue Light' (Cann, Cross, Currie, Foxx, Simon) 3:09

Ultravox does disco? Not quite, but 'Blue Light' does verge on it. Self-aware, the lyrics admit, 'There was something wrong/But I couldn't quite put my finger on it'. The goodwill supplied by the out-of-the-gate 'Slow Motion' and 'I Can't Stay Long' was wilting by this point, the energy drifting away as Foxx got caught up in shouting and random lyrics. There's a marked decline in quality and innovation as side one creaks to a close.

'Some Of Them' (Currie, Foxx) 2:29

This redeems things somewhat, even if it's a clear throwback to the more punky *Ha!-Ha!-Ha!*. It's short, sharp, and doesn't outstay its welcome, yet it feels like a leftover from an earlier time.

'Quiet Men' (Cross, Currie, Foxx) 4:08

The best material beyond the album's opening two tracks appears on side two. 'This was another song which we knew had that *special something* about it', admitted Cann. Foxx's singing gives life to a work that originated as poetry in his then-unpublished collection of short stories *The Quiet Man*. Foxx's stories followed the exploits of a mysterious observer figure who explores a series of seemingly parallel worlds. Throughout his early songwriting – but especially on *Systems Of Romance* and his solo debut *Metamatic* – Foxx repurposed some of that material, turning the poems/ short stories into songs (as with 'Quiet Men'). Themes explored on this album included the dissolution, fusion or fragmentation of identity ('I Can't Stay Long': 'When the right time comes, I'll dissolve') and memory as a place that can be revisited ('Slow Motion': 'Pictures, I've got pictures/And I run them in my head' and 'Some Of Them': 'Some of them live in photographs'). It made for a rich stew Foxx could pull images and metaphors from to form his evocative but obscure lyrics. The later Midge Ure-fronted Ultravox would tackle similar material but from a much more commercial direction with yet more songs about movies, dancing and the troubles of youth.

'Quiet Men' exhibits the same approach that worked well on 'Slow Motion'. Guitar and electronics are given equal prominence. There's the icy coldness of the mechanical rhythms and heavy synth use that would come to define electropop in the early 1980s. Simon's lively guitar riff also gives the track warmth and a human touch. Currie again delivers a solid synth solo, something that would become even more of a trademark in the Ure era.

In *Record Mirror*, Tim Lott branded the single as 'English pop with Germanic synthetic discipline. Insistent repeat pulse, electric percussion ... Good enough to avoid the charts!'.

This was the album's second single, released on 20 October 1978, with 'Cross Fade' as the B-side. There was also 'Quiet Men (Full)' (running time 3:55) released, but it failed to make any impression on the UK charts. It took Ultravox admirer Gary Numan to take a sound like 'Quiet Men' to the top of the charts in 1979 with 'Cars'.

'Dislocation' (Currie, Foxx) 2:55

Despite the sounds here, no drum machine was used, a fact Warren Cann was rather proud of. The sounds that form the rhythm were achieved by what Cann characterised as the 'painstaking maltreatment' of Currie's ARP synthesizer. It almost anticipates what Depeche Mode would be doing four years later when they entered their *metal-bashing* phase inspired by German experimental group Einstürzende Neubauten. As ever, Ultravox got there first, yet their pioneering achievements were all but ignored at the time. 1978 – when *Systems Of Romance* was released – was the height of disco's popularity. The John Foxx version of Ultravox failed to surf the emerging new wave. While their work anticipated many of the sounds and lyrical concerns of the New Romantics and early-1980s electropop, Ultravox arrived too early to capitalise on it. Instead, Foxx and Ultravox had to settle for being unsung pioneers who would only be recognised in retrospect as having anticipated so much of the music style that was to come over the next few years.

'Dislocation' sounds like nothing else from 1978, with lyrics anticipating the band's later 'Mr. X':

Someone came into the room while I was half asleep
We spoke for a while
I couldn't see his face
Later on when he was gone
I realised I didn't catch his name

The track was also the B-side to 'Slow Motion': an ideal sonic pairing.

'Maximum Acceleration' (Foxx) 3:53

This Foxx song, anticipating his future work on *Metamatic* and beyond, again fuses guitars and drums with exquisite synth work. An almost soulful vocal makes the track stand out, proving that if he'd really wanted to, Foxx could've been a huge pop star in the style of ABC or Spandau Ballet. However, he couldn't help himself – while the delivery hides it a bit, the lyric is as obscure as ever. It's another track that Gary Numan seems to have paid close attention to. Compare it with his 'Conversation' from *The Pleasure Principal*. Ironically, in the break between the Foxx and Ure incarnations of Ultravox, Billy Currie played on Numan's *Pleasure Principal* tour.

'When You Walk Through Me' (Currie, Foxx, Simon) 4:15

With an opening that subtly anticipates 'All Stood Still' or 'Sleepwalk', this track melds the earlier punk-rock approach with electronic sounds and Conny Plank's muscular production. Cann later admitted to using the drum pattern from The Beatles' 'Tomorrow Never Knows' as a homage but claimed that no one ever spotted it. Certainly, some of Foxx's fascination with Beatles-style psychedelia might've rubbed off on the drummer.

'Just For A Moment' (Currie, Foxx) 3:10

As with 'Dislocation', the rhythm track came from Cann torturing Currie's ARP Odyssey synthesizer to create a variety of percussive effects centring on a heartbeat motif. As with the two previous albums, *Systems Of Romance* ends on a slow, downbeat, heavily electronic track that disentangles the DNA that made up the band. Currie's solo piano playing interrupts the cold, melancholy electronics, giving life to this electro ballad.

The lyric line 'Listening to the music the machines make' not only defined Ultravox's ethos but became the title of Richard Evans' 2022 history of electronic pop music covering the years 1978 to 1983. As Warren Cann reflected, by the time of *Systems Of Romance*, 'We were firmly in the first stages of becoming truly comfortable … as it was our third album, we were now also becoming familiar with the feeling of knowing we'd have to top ourselves with each subsequent release, and it occasionally began to weigh upon us'. At that point, driving force John Foxx decided to quit the band.

Related Tracks

'Cross Fade' (Cann, Cross, Currie, Foxx) 2:53

Relegated to the B-side of 'Quiet Men', 'Cross Fade' was strong enough to be on the album, perhaps in place of a clunker like 'Blue Light' or 'Some Of Them'. Thudding percussion and a strong high-toned synth line dominate, with Foxx all but shouting the programmatic vocal. The usual obsessions surface – driving, drowning, flicker and film: all encapsulated in the final lines, 'Pictures into structures and structures into motion/Cross over into action, over airways, over ocean'.

'Radio Beach' (Live) (Foxx) 3:47

An unreleased track that was never recorded, this is a song Warren Cann has no recollection of. It was never played live in the UK but was part of the 1979 US setlist along with three other songs that later emerged on Foxx solo albums – 'He's A Liquid' and 'Touch And Go' (*Metamatic*), and 'Systems Of Romance': obviously written for this album but left out, later surfacing on Foxx's *The Garden*. Given the band played these songs live on that US tour, they can be considered as Ultravox tracks. 'Radio Beach' is the curious omission, existing alongside other lost Foxx-era Ultravox songs like 'TV Orphans', 'Dark Love', 'City Doesn't Care', and 'Car Crash Flashback', which from its Ballardian title alone sounds like it belonged on a Foxx album.

'Radio Beach' was never demoed (which the other tracks were, in anticipation of a fourth Foxx Ultravox album), but it did surface on YouTube in a poor live recording from 4 March 1979 in Buffalo. Opening with a long synth drone, the song has something of *Vienna*'s 'New Europeans' about it. Foxx claimed in a live introduction that this was 'a song about Blackpool beach in England: the Golden Mile, where you can't see the sand for all the transistor radios'.

'He's A Liquid' (Live) (Foxx) 6:00

A further four songs were played live on the 1978-79 American tour that later appeared on Foxx solo albums (often in a different form). Having never been recorded, only ropey live recordings from that tour are available.

At the 2 March 1979 gig at Boston's Paradise Theatre, Foxx introduced 'He's A Liquid' as being 'a new song, about how people get changed due to the pressures that surround them, just like a liquid'. Heavier on guitar than the *Metamatic* version; it's longer than the album version and contains significantly different lyrics. There's a notable instrumental middle section with significant input from guitarist Robin Simon and Billy Currie on violin, anticipating later *Rage In Eden* tracks.

'Touch And Go' (Live) (Foxx) 5:39

This song also appeared on 1980's *Metamatic*, and heavily influenced the later Ultravox track 'Mr. X' (as did parts of 'He's A Liquid'). Introducing the song live, Foxx said it was 'about the kind of life that we lead'.

While the backing rhythm is clearly that used on the subsequent Ultravox track 'Mr. X', the singing and lyrics are very different from Foxx's minimal *Metamatic* version. As with 'He's A Liquid', Billy Currie cuts loose with his violin in a way not reflected on the Foxx studio recording, but that does anticipate some of his dramatic playing on *Rage In Eden*.

The track ends with some instrumental noodling that echoes 'Mr. X', though the live and studio versions of 'Touch And Go' lack the distinctive film-noir atmosphere that 'Mr. X' ultimately received, especially with Warren Cann's vocals. Whether there was any formal agreement between the parties when

Foxx's Ultravox disintegrated is unclear, but both subsequent musical entities moved in different – if somewhat compatible – directions, as 'Touch And Go' and 'Mr. X' reveal.

'Walk Away' (Live) (Foxx) 3:42
This song was quickly dropped from the live set but resurfaced on Foxx's second solo album *The Garden* (which featured by-then-former Ultravox guitarist Robin Simon). Driven by guitar and drums more than the previous two tracks, it's something of a punk throwback, which might be why they dropped it, given the direction they were moving in. Again, Foxx later heavily overhauled the lyric.

This live track builds to a cacophony before collapsing in on itself, crashing to a definitive halt. For the studio version, things took a cleaner, more electronic turn, though it features a Currie-style piano part (obviously not by him), resulting in a calmer version. It seems that while generating new material in his solo career, Foxx couldn't let go of these earlier songs. It does appear that the band had no intention of splitting up on that tour and were, in fact, developing new material, presumably in anticipation of recording a fourth album, though Island Records *had* dropped them by this point. Whatever actually went on, it seemed Foxx couldn't simply entirely walk away from Ultravox.

'Systems Of Romance' (Foxx) 4:04
Though the third Island album was titled *Systems Of Romance*, the song of the same title didn't make the cut. A later track with that title surfaced on Foxx's second solo album *The Garden*. It seems that 'Systems Of Romance' dates from the same touring period as the live tracks, or perhaps earlier during the recording of the third album. It's certainly the most Ultravox-sounding track on *The Garden* (along with the curiously titled 'Dancing Like A Gun'). The album title *Systems Of Romance* was said to have been inspired by producer Conny Plank's interest in the systems music of such minimalists as Philip Glass, Steve Reich and Michael Nyman. The core of systems music was mathematical musical progress across an extended time period. Foxx said: 'I like the idea of intangible emotional elements running through mathematical frameworks. It seemed a perfect encapsulation of the spirit of the music I was attempting to get to at the moment'.

Vienna (1980)

Personnel:
Midge Ure: lead vocals, guitars, synthesizers
Warren Cann: drums, electronic percussion, backing vocals, lead vocals on 'Mr. X' ('Herr X')
Billy Currie: violin, viola, piano, synthesizers
Chris Cross: bass, synthesizers, backing vocals
Producers: Conny Plank, Ultravox
Recorded at RAK (London), February 1980
Label: Chrysalis
Release date: 11 July 1980 (UK)
Charts: UK: 3, US: 164, AUS: 4, BEL: 1, CAN: 80, NL: 1, Germany: 22, JAP: 79, NZ: 2, NOR: 18, SW: 6
Running time: 43:37

Though Island Records dropped Ultravox after the perceived failure of *Systems Of Romance* (in sales terms, at least), there was no indication the band would fall apart. It certainly came as a surprise to Warren Cann, as he told Jonas Warstad: 'We certainly weren't pumping out chart-topping hits. Still, our actual sales seemed to be making progress, and we felt we were just on the verge of success'. That slow progress wasn't enough for Island, who terminated the contract on the final day of 1978. It seemed that Ultravox – being several years ahead of the curve, musically speaking – didn't fit any niche. They were not punk, disco, or rock 'n' roll, but some hybrid. Also, the band had no support from the UK music press, which equally seemed at a loss to categorise their music, though there *were* some perceptive exceptions.

Perhaps it was Foxx's final roll of the dice, but the band self-funded a US tour in 1979, playing several new songs, suggesting they were planning a new album despite being without a recording contract. It must've been all the more surprising – especially to Currie and Cann – when, in the spring of 1979, Ultravox crumbled.

Their final gig with Foxx took place at Hollywood's Whisky a Go Go in March 1979. The roots of his departure went back further than that. The *Systems Of Romance* track 'I Can't Stay Long' contained the telling lines, 'I can't stay long/When the right time comes, I'll resign'. In a 2020 interview with *The Quietus*, Foxx admitted:

> I'd actually written 'I Can't Stay Long' at the same time as 'Hiroshima Mon Amour' in 1977. I decided to leave the band during rehearsals for *Systems* in London before we went to Germany to record. The line went in the song at that point. The strain in the band was entirely down to me wanting to be free. The entire final US tour became difficult ... I didn't dislike the band at all, but all the touring and travelling burnt me out. The serious psychic drain of performing every night reduced me to a numb ghost.

Foxx saw an opportunity in the new technology they'd been exploring, from various synthesizers and drum machines to new multitrack recording equipment. The creation of 'Hiroshima Mon Amour' had opened Foxx's eyes to the possibility that a solo act – one *quiet man* alone – could use technology to produce quality music: a blending of man and machine as he'd conceived in 'I Want To Be A Machine'. Foxx had only one regret about quitting: leaving Robin Simon behind (suggesting he'd failed to appreciate exactly what Billy Currie had contributed to the band). Simon also left the group in order to stay in the US after meeting and marrying Grace Weisbard in 1979. He settled in Coney Island, New York, and soon joined The Futants before eventually returning to England to play with Magazine.

By April 1979, all that remained of Ultravox was Currie, Cann, and Cross. They had no record label and no vocalist and were down one guitarist. According to Cann, the trio were 'determined to keep the band alive'. They set out to find a lead guitarist who was also a singer. Upon returning from the ill-fated US tour, the ever-industrious Currie worked with Rich Kids drummer Rusty Egan on what eventually became Visage.

Also involved in that studio-based project (with Steve Strange as frontman) was former Rich Kids member Midge Ure. At Egan's suggestion, Currie approached Ure about possibly joining Ultravox. Glasgow-born James 'Midge' Ure had already experienced considerable musical success in various bands since 1969 (when he was aged 16). He played guitar in Glasgow band Stumble before joining Salvation in 1972, playing with brothers Kenny and Jim McGinlay. As Ure was also known as Jim, he adopted the nickname 'Midge', being a phonetic reversal of Jim (Mij) to differentiate him from McGinlay. The name stuck. By 1974 with the departure of Kenny McGinlay, Ure took over singing for Salvation, who then changed their name to Slik. The Slik songs were written by Bay City Rollers' songwriters Bill Martin and Phil Coulter.

While finding his feet as a vocalist, Ure had been approached by Malcolm McLaren, looking for a singer to front the Sex Pistols: an opportunity Ure declined. It proved to be the right decision when Slik scored a number one UK single (knocking ABBA off the top spot) with Bay City Rollers' soundalike glam-rock song 'Forever And Ever' in February 1976. Readers of *The Sun* voted Slik the 'best new band' of the year. Their second top 40 hit 'Requiem' followed in May, though it peaked at 24. (Opening line: 'It's over, we've come to the end now'!). Slik disbanded in September 1977 in the face of the more-aggressive punk movement. (Ure's one attempt at punk was PVC2 – a rebranded Slik – whose track 'Put You In The Picture' was recorded in an empty pub!)

When bass player Glen Matlock quit the Sex Pistols in 1977, he formed Rich Kids, recruiting Steve New (lead guitar), Rusty Egan (drums), and Midge Ure (guitar, keyboards, lead vocals). Their sole top 40 single 'Rich Kids' reached 24 in the UK (curiously, matching 'Requiem'). Rich Kids soon fell apart when Ure and Egan declared an interest in pursuing electronic music.

That led them to Visage and their number eight hit 'Fade To Grey', and the two albums *Visage* and *The Anvil*. Ure also toured the US as a member of Thin Lizzy in 1979, making an impact with the Ure/Lynott co-write 'Yellow Pearl' (1980), which was the theme to the UK pop show *Top Of The Pops* between 1981 and 1986.

Cann described the band getting to know Ure, which involved sessions in the pub and casual rehearsals to see how they gelled: 'He truly was an excellent guitarist, something usually overlooked in assessments of him. And he could sing, as opposed to shout-with-attitude. With no reservations, we resolved that we'd found the right person to complete the new lineup, and Midge was in.'

By autumn 1979, the new foursome were working on new material. Among the first tracks completed were the instrumental 'Astradyne', 'New Europeans', 'Western Promise', and 'All Stood Still', all of which would appear on *Vienna*. A US tour followed in December 1979, playing a mix of this new material, Foxx-era songs like 'Dislocation', 'Quiet Men', 'Slow Motion' and 'Hiroshima Mon Amour', and drawing on each member's new wider experience (primarily Currie's with Gary Numan and in Visage).

Upon returning to the UK, Ultravox signed to Chrysalis Records, and set to work creating *Vienna*. Recorded in just ten days (in stark contrast to the three-month process that would follow on *Rage In Eden*) at RAK in London, *Vienna* was mixed in two weeks at Conny Plank's Cologne studio.

Released in July 1980, *Vienna* was the first Ultravox album to reach the UK album chart, entering at 14 after one week. By the end of 1980, Ultravox had transformed from a non-charting but critically acclaimed band with a solid fan base into essentially a new band capable of producing significant hits. That was the view of Billy Currie: '*Vienna* was the start of a new group; we're more of a unit now. We've done all that touring together. When we get an idea, we seem to click together straight away'. All four *Vienna* singles had made their mark on the charts, with 'Sleepwalk' reaching 29. The follow-up 'Passing Strangers' had disappointed, stalling at 57. The title track 'Vienna' was the true breakthrough, hitting number two. The album's final single 'All Stood Still' also crashed the top ten, hitting number eight. The album itself reached number three, selling in excess of 300,000, going Platinum and spending an astounding 72 weeks in the chart.

Despite this popularity, the album was met with a mixed critical reaction. In *Record Mirror*, Phil Hall wrote that though 'Ultravox make all the right noises, they are never capable of writing consistently memorable pieces ... *Vienna* is full of conventional electronic rock songs, which are beautifully executed but never inspiring'. *Smash Hits'* Steve Taylor said Midge Ure had changed the band for the better, and he'd 'done these leading lights of electropop nothing but good', awarding *Vienna* eight out of ten stars, describing the album as 'synthesizer music with backbone and muscle'. In *Sounds*, John Gill was equally positive: 'I dare you to find another band who can mix Euro systems rock, electronics, Can's fairground style and English music, with such panache'. *NME*'s Chris Bonn was more equivocal, saying *Vienna* was 'an album of gaudy, sometimes magnificent, but mostly hollow edifices, housing songs that replace Foxx's elliptical imagery with clumsily verbose descriptions of similar scenery … seemingly derived from Hollywood films … it's similarly full of glamour and lacking in true essence … Despite their wanton plagiarism and less-clearly-defined ideas, *Vienna* will probably be the album that makes Ultravox'. While pointing out some of the album's weaknesses (being mainly a lack of humour), Penny Kiley in *Melody Maker* presciently declared, 'Ultravox deserve success. This should do the trick'.

'Astradyne' (Cann, Cross, Currie, Ure) 7:07

Electropop bands often featured instrumentals on their albums. Kraftwerk tracks were often light on vocals, while the first Depeche Mode album *Speak & Spell* (1981) featured Martin Gore's 'Big Muff', while Gary Numan's *Replicas* (1979) featured the instrumentals 'When The Machines Rock' and 'I Nearly Married A Human' (which together ran for over nine minutes). Frenchman Jean-Michel Jarre was releasing entirely instrumental electronic albums. Across the previous three Ultravox albums, there was no purely instrumental track, so it was a positively brave move for the new incarnation to open their debut with a seven-minute instrumental. (The track closed side one of the US issue.)

As a statement of intent, 'Astradyne' employed almost every synth the band had available, from the Roland CR-78 CompuRhythm drum machine (a setting called 'Metal Beat', later used as a Foxx title on *Metamatic*), live drums, bass, Yamaha CP70 electric piano, Yamaha SS30 string machine, Minimoog and ARP Odyssey. The combination became the signature Ultravox sound.

Driven by Ure, the band were experimenting with several tracks that lacked lyrics. Warren Cann recalled: 'There was one instrumental piece that Midge had brought in, which we played about with for some time … but for some reason, it never really came together and we dropped it. Midge reprised the idea with Phil Lynott, and it became 'Yellow Pearl''. Also a product of these early sessions, Cann dubbed 'Astradyne' as 'certainly exciting'. The piece was initially titled 'Ad Astra', from the Latin phrase 'Per ardua ad astra': the RAF motto, meaning 'Through struggle, to the stars'. Somewhere along the way, this morphed into 'Astradyne': a curious mix of Latin and Greek which roughly means 'star power'. The 'dyne' part may have come from US rocket engine company Rocketdyne.

The track is a slow burn, building from seemingly random sounds into a coherent piece of classical-inspired electropop. Each instrument takes its place in the overall mix, creating a sweeping, majestic sound with time to explore. It was a rousing concert opener, especially on the 21st-century reunion tours and at Midge Ure's 70th birthday celebration concert at the Royal Albert Hall in October 2023.

'New Europeans' (Cann, Cross, Currie, Ure) 4:01

Given that Ultravox were considered to be a synth band at the forefront of
the new wave of electronic pop, it's a revelation how guitar-driven much of
Vienna actually is – no track more so than this first to feature Midge Ure on
vocals. This perception of Ultravox was reinforced by lines like 'His modern
world revolves around the synthesizer's song'. Immediately, it starts with
prominent guitar and drums: the very antithesis of the likes of Gary Numan.
It hits the chorus before the distinct 'synthesiser's song' kicks in. It was
especially good when played live.

The lyrics are not far removed from those of John Foxx, with media references,
from 'lies pressed in magazines' to 'his brand new radio'; from 'his television's
in his bed' to 'he's frozen to the screen'. Even the new concept of the portable
Walkman 'headphones' gets a mention. The heartbeat-backed final verse is an
anomaly. It's a transitional track, starting strong with guitars and drums but
resolving in a deluge of synths and electric piano courtesy of Billy Currie.

According to the 40th-anniversary deluxe box-set liner notes, the title
preceded the song. (They usually wrote music first.) The track was used
for a whisky advertisement in Japan, resulting in huge popularity for the
band there when it was released as a Japan-only single, with 'Vienna' on the
B-side. (The bizarrely translated lyric on the sleeve is a hoot, however: 'a
mystic in soul food' indeed!) At a formal Japanese ceremony, the band were
presented with a gold record, marking their significant sales in the territory.
'It was a memorable moment', said the deadpan Cann.

'Private Lives' (Cann, Cross, Currie, Ure) 4:06

A piano motif begins 'Private Lives', as mere seconds in the synths are front-
and-centre, ably supported by Cann's drumming. Like 'Artificial Life', this
reads like a Blitz club song: 'We dance till dawn as they beat the drums'.
The opening lines capture the atmosphere of an early-1980s club night,
with everyone done up in New Romantic finery: 'All the boys are wearing
blue tonight', 'All the strangers walk like you tonight'. Currie arranged the
instrumental section in homage to a 1960s Steppenwolf album, with guitar
lines played in reverse. Currie said in the liner notes: 'This has some voice
screeches (sounding like squealing brakes) from Chris Cross. These were
done to edit on the end of the sustaining guitar note that comes out of
the middle piano solo. When the guitar pulls off, it slides down and stops
abruptly. The voice screech was edited on the end of that'. The opening
piano section was often played much slower in concert, with the vocal
screech stretched out even further.

'Passing Strangers' (Cann, Cross, Currie, Ure) 3:48

The second single (released on 15 October 1980) failed to match the top
30 success of 'Sleepwalk', stalling at a rather poor 57. That's all the more
astonishing, considering the brilliant video that Chrysalis funded. It was

shot at London's abandoned Beckton Gas Works (which operated between 1870 and 1976), once the largest in Europe. It was a popular film location, used in episodes of Michael Bentine's *It's A Square World* in the 1960s, in the 1975 John Wayne film *Brannigan* and in the opening of the 1981 James Bond movie *For Your Eyes Only*. The 1985 *Max Headroom* TV movie *20 Minutes Into The Future* (which Ure and Cross wrote the theme for) was also shot there.

The video was directed by Australian Russell Mulcahy (director of *Highlander* (1986)) and featured future *Hellbound: Hellraiser II* star Barbie Wilde. (She played Female Cenobite.) She'd studied classical mime and formed the rock-burlesque troupe SHOCK, which supported various bands in the late 1970s and early 1980s, including Ultravox at The Rainbow in 1981, Adam and the Ants, Depeche Mode, Gary Numan, and Classix Nouveaux. In the video, her partner – seemingly on the run from oppressive forces (represented by the band members) across a desolate post-industrial world – was robotic mime artist Tok, Sean Crawford from duo Tik & Tok. They were also part of SHOCK and recorded the single 'Angel Face' (produced by Visage's Rusty Egan) with Wilde.

It's a brilliant short film, opening with solarised images of desolate industry. The black-and-white clip sees the male and female figures awakening through robotic movements (are they *Blade Runner*-style *replicants*, humanoid robots, or perhaps a life form persecuted in this dystopia?) to more fluid human movements as they go on the run. The magical moment when they kiss and the video bursts into colour with a dramatic explosion is genius. Why this video didn't drive single sales is a mystery, although this was before MTV and saturation video rotation, so the only outlets on UK TV then would've been *Top Of The Pops*, a few Saturday-morning kids shows and the few other music shows then on air. The video gave the new Ultravox an instant image, carried through in Brian Griffin's photography adorning the *Vienna* album sleeve. The sharp black-and-white images of the band with Ure holding his hands out robot-style – complete with Clark Gable moustache and undone bow tie – set a clear new wave trend edging towards a New Romantic theme.

'Passing Strangers' is a fast guitar-and-drums-driven track that boasts enough electronics to differentiate it from earlier Foxx-era Ultravox sounds.

'Sleepwalk' (Cann, Cross, Currie, Ure) 3:10

The album's first single was Ultravox's first top 30 hit, reaching 29 in August 1980. As part of their new deal with Chrysalis, the band opted to record a master version of 'Sleepwalk' (at RAK Studios in February 1980) rather than record a demo as was still traditional. They had a high degree of confidence in the new material, as they'd written much of it in late 1979 and road-tested it on the December 1979 US tour and early 1980 UK dates. Producer Conny Plank was retained from *Systems Of Romance*, and the finished 'Sleepwalk' secured the Chrysalis deal.

The writer credit for this song lists all four band members, and Warren Cann wrote the lyric, continuing to have a hand in lyrics across the next two albums. Cann noted:

> One of the most refreshing aspects of our new band was that we all accredited ourselves as writers. We were adamant there was to be no more arguing over who was or wasn't responsible for what. In this healthy and equitable climate, ideas passed far more freely ... we would all make suggestions towards each other's contributions – so much so, in fact, that the only possible financial arrangement regarding the writing was to split everything equally. It was a very sensible arrangement but a rarity amongst bands. It ensured that whatever else we might argue over in future days, it would never be over money. It proved to be true for the lifespan of the group.

'Sleepwalk' was a short, sharp blast of punk-infused new wave. Not as fast as 'ROckWrok', there is nonetheless something of the old punk Ultravox in its synth-driven make-up. The middle break gave Currie a chance to develop his soon-to-be trademark keyboard solos.

Hitting the top 30 got Ultravox onto *Top Of The Pops* for the first time (the Foxx-era Ultravox had played the late-night BBC2 alternative *The Old Grey Whistle Test*). This was far from a first for Midge Ure, who'd appeared at least three times with Slik alone, but Billy Currie certainly seemed determined to make the most of it with his waggling backside stealing the show.

'Sleepwalk' was a track that could've easily suited *Systems Of Romance*, even if the lyric was simpler, if no-less obscure. Cann said, 'It reflected a stylistic change because Midge's singing was very different from John Foxx's, plus Midge was the best guitarist we'd ever had ... Still, we kept following the areas of sound that excited us. The chemistry within the band was now very different, but it enabled Bill, Chris and myself to enjoy ourselves much more'.

The single won an enthusiastic notice from *Smash Hits*: 'An attractive dance tune in infectious fashion ... streamlined enough to get on the radio'. The single spent seven weeks in the top 40, helped by radio airplay and the band's debut *Top Of The Pops* appearance.

'Mr. X' (Cann, Cross, Currie, Ure) 6:33

In the *Vienna* deluxe-edition liner notes, Warren Cann said, 'If anyone is wondering what this song is about, I can at least tell them it's certainly not about John Foxx or Bowie or any number of other candidates I've been asked about'. A track full of mystery, 'Mr. X' sounds like Kraftwerk (specifically like an escapee from *The Man-Machine*), except for Cann's resonant spoken film-noir narrative. In fact, this obviously recalls the slower, colder Foxx-era tracks like 'My Sex' and 'Hiroshima Mon Amour', with Cann stepping in for Foxx (something that would've never happened then). The electronic ambience is packed with dark tones and laden with Cold War atmospheres, with the narrative hinting at an unsolved mystery. 'Mr. X' revealed that the new Ultravox could smoothly swing from the guitar-driven pop of 'New Europeans' and 'Passing Strangers' to the Numan/Kraftwerk likes of this. Right in the middle of the six-minute runtime, up pops Currie with another of his trademark violin solos: not the kind of thing most bands then featured.

'Western Promise' (Cann, Cross, Currie, Ure) 5:18
'Mr. X' cross-fades directly into 'Western Promise': a technique that would get much more use on the following album *Rage In Eden*.

Warren Cann recorded his drums for this track in the studio's public vestibule in the middle of the night because 'the surroundings were all glass and polished marble: excellent for a *hard* drum sound'. The propulsive drumming alarmed the residents of St. John's Wood. Slashing minor chords cut through, swamped by sweeping Giorgio Moroder-style synths. Visage-like vocals and Ure's cries of 'Hai!' cut in. The final line plays like they just gave up: 'All minions to Messiah Pepsi can'. Despite that, this was the album's most energetic track. It also cross-fades directly into the next track.

'Vienna' (Cann, Cross, Currie, Ure) 4:53
The third of the album's four singles, 'Vienna' (released 9 January 1981) was a different sound, much slower than prior singles 'Sleepwalk' and 'Passing Strangers' and the raucous follow-up 'All Stood Still'.

The track was something of a Frankenstein, built in January 1980 from a free-floating chorus line and a rhythm pattern Warren Cann had been developing (connected to the opening of 'Astradyne'). Ure had the beginnings of a lyric: 'The feeling is gone'. Currie pulled this all together in the style of a late-19th-century romantic composer like Greig or Elgar, with his violin solo inspired by German composer Max Reger. Currie told *Electronic Sound*: 'That was something I really wanted to do. I wanted to bring classical into electronic music, which was quite unusual at that time'. The resulting orchestration was initially not to Ure's taste, Currie claiming the singer said, 'This means nothing to me'. Conny Plank then suggested that it should become a vocal line, which resulted in the lines: 'The feeling is gone/Only you and I/It means nothing to me/This means nothing to me/Oh Vienna'. Ure denied this story on Twitter in 2021.

As for the song's meaning, the track and video offer some intriguing clues. When faced with the dreaded *inspirations* question in early interviews, Ure had a ready-made answer – the song was inspired by the 1949 film-noir movie *The Third Man*, which starred Joseph Cotten and Orson Welles and was set in Vienna. He later admitted to *Rolling Stone* that this was *not* the basis of the song: 'I lied to the papers ... I'd written a song about a holiday romance, but in this very dark, ominous surrounding'. Ure talked to *The*

Guardian in 2017: "'Vienna' was a love song to an imaginary girl. You've gone to this beautiful place, met someone, and vowed it is going to continue, and of course, it doesn't. Why Vienna? There was a decaying elegance about it. In such a crumbling environment, you could easily fall in love'.

Ure later added another inspiration: The Walker Brothers' 1978 song 'The Electrician', supposedly about CIA-funded torture in the 1970s right-wing regimes of Chile and Argentina. Talk about dark and ominous. There are structural similarities, though the two tracks are fundamentally different. Ure said, 'We wanted to take the song and make it incredibly pompous in the middle, leaving it very sparse before and after, but finishing with a typically over-the-top classical ending'.

The lengthy instrumental break was – like much of the track – anti-pop music, playing out a classical-sounding track in an electronic style. Few others were quite doing this at that time. The instrumental combination, enigmatic lyric, forceful vocal and climax combined to make the first listen to 'Vienna' an unforgettable and disorienting moment. It quickly became their signature song and was – inevitably – much mocked while still being fondly remembered by those who bought it the first time around.

The song's wasn't an obvious choice for a single. Currie told *The Guardian*: 'When we heard the final mix, we didn't think we had a hit. It was just a track. Others seemed just as likely to chart, such as 'Mr. X'. But I wanted to release it. I was proud of it and couldn't bear the thought of it being passed over'.

Ure told *The Guardian*: 'The label didn't want to put 'Vienna' out. It was too slow, too long, and there was a violin solo: the antithesis of a commercial single. Then, the moment it became huge, the pressure on us to surpass it with a follow-up was incredible. Everyone wanted us to write a track called 'Berlin' or 'Paris''.

Two memorable features are attached to 'Vienna' – the groundbreaking music video, and the fact it was held at number two in the UK and kept from the top spot for four weeks, first by John Lennon's 'Woman', and then the Joe Dolce novelty record 'Shaddap You Face' which had been climbing the charts slowly behind 'Vienna'. Roxy Music's 'Jealous Guy' (written by Lennon) and Adam and the Ants' 'Kings Of The Wild Frontier' then pushed 'Vienna' down to number four. 'Vienna' had a 14-week run in the UK top 40, peaking at number two, spending eight weeks in the top ten and 11 in the top 20. It landed at number six on the UK's best-selling singles of 1981, selling in excess of 500,000. Cann noted: 'We were very proud of that, and it went some considerable way towards making up for never having gotten to number one'. 'Vienna' was the only number two song in the year's top nine, beaten into the top five by Shakin' Stevens' 'This Ole House'. Bassist Chris Cross later said of the Joe Dolce track: 'It annoyed Midge at the time. This is going to sound terrible, but I quite like that song; I think it's funny'. In 2013, 'Vienna' was named the UK's favourite number two single in a poll by Radio 2 and the Official Charts Company and was given an honorary number one award.

The distinctive video was a labour of love, cementing the group's apparent European, futurist sensibilities with a healthy dose of the neo-Romantic past thrown in. After 'Passing Strangers', Chrysalis refused to fund another video, especially for a track they thought to be too slow, long and dour, with a weird violin solo in the middle. Instead, the band initially funded the video, again by Russell Mulcahy. It cost £7000. Many of the evocative and seemingly foreign locations were actually in central London, including around Covent Garden and at the old Kilburn Gaumont Theatre. The Vienna location shoot involved the band and a cameraman flying out for a weekend (accompanied by Paula Yates, who wrote about the shoot in *Record Mirror* in February 1981), snatching shots of historic-looking places. According to Cann: 'We took an early-morning flight to Vienna, ran 'round like loonies in and out of taxis as we filmed … We finished up in the cemetery for the shots with the statue, which had been used for the single's cover (a gentleman – Carl Schweighofer – who made pianos for the rich and famous of his time), did the sunset shot, and then dashed back to London to start editing'.

The video tells a story, seemingly of some 18th-century romantic intrigue, with multiple denizens of the Blitz club playing aristocrats gathered at a party, including filmmaker Julien Temple (with the spider on his face). While Ure warbles from the sidelines, the other band members appear as news photographers and then as diplomats delivering gossip to an important aristocratic figure. The whole thing ends in a violent shooting, with dashes of surrealism throughout, just to throw some confusion into the otherwise straightforward narrative. The video set a trend for flashy, story-driven, often obscure pop-music videos, lasting throughout much of the 1980s.

Being a stone-cold classic of its era, 'Vienna' is the most-used Ultravox track by TV and film producers – from a 1996 episode of sporting-rivalries documentary series *Clash Of The Titans* (Episode Three: 'Phoenix From The Ashes'), right up to the 2021 crashed-schoolgirls cannibalism drama *Yellowjackets* (Season One, Episode Three: 'The Dollhouse' and Season One, Episode Ten: 'Sic Transit Gloria Mundi'). In between, the track was heard in the 2005 detective movie *Quo Vadis, Baby?*, in two episodes of 1980s nostalgia drama *Ashes To Ashes* (2008), the 2009 1980s nostalgia documentaries *Electric Dreams* and *Synth Britannia*, US drama series *The Americans* (2015), *13 Reasons Why* (2017), *American Crime Story* (2018), and even popped up in episodes of *The Crown* and *Doctor Who* ('Cold War' (2013), in which David Warner plays an Ultravox fan on a Russian submarine).

According to Billy Currie in *Smash Hits,* it was 'the right time for 'Vienna' … It feels just right for us, this moody European sound'. The final word on 'Vienna' goes to Midge Ure in the 1984 fan book *Ultravox: In Their Own Words*: 'Our music is quite grand. We like things to be overblown, and we do it for a reason. 'Vienna' was very tongue-in-cheek, we thought it was funny, but nobody got it. Everybody read too much into it. It would be nice for someone to pick up in ten years and still remember it'.

'All Stood Still' (Cann, Cross, Currie, Ure) 4:21
The album's fourth and final single 'All Stood Still' (released on 28 May 1981) wasn't that clever a choice after the magisterial 'Vienna'. It did give the band their second top-ten hit, peaking at eight. Ure noted: 'This was all built around the Moog bass line and resulted in a great synth/guitar riff – very techno-metal!'. It's certainly an over-the-top summation of everything *Vienna* was attempting – a perfect blend of guitar and drums with epic synth lines, played at a whopping speed even outstripping 'Western Promise'. The nervous energy was unleashed, propelling this forward, with the near-shouted vocals screaming about the end of the world. It wasn't though – just the end of this album.

Related Tracks
'Waiting' (Cann, Cross, Currie, Ure) 3:51
The 'Sleepwalk' B-side is altogether more subdued. There's a hint of Visage in the instrumentation (like an off-cut from *The Anvil*) and a hint of the early Eno/Roxy Music influences, though retooled for the new wave era. More an ambient/spoken-word piece (in the style of 'Mr. X') than a proper song, 'Waiting' was too out-of-keeping with the driving attitude of *Vienna* to be included.

Opening slowly, the song rides along to a marching rhythm, reflected in the lyric: 'Move on as we step in time', 'Syncopate with the marching song'. It anticipates a battle to come, perhaps awaiting the order to go 'over the top' in the trenches of World War I. 'Thoughts and dreams flick across your mind/Fade away as you wait for your time to go/You're waiting, waiting, waiting'. Spacey instrumental effects and washes intersperse with the strictly regimented chorus and verse structure, and the track drifts off into a final fade, washing away.

'Passionate Reply' (Cann, Cross, Currie, Ure) 4:17
A track which might've felt right at home on *Vienna*, 'Passionate Reply' was the 'Vienna' B-side, and recorded separately from the rest of the album. In August 1980, during the US tour, the band booked Criteria Studios in Miami in response to a request from Chrysalis to record a B-side. According to Cann, it was 'a promising song; perhaps it needed some living with before we would've considered it finished. As it was, we thought it made a good B-side'. Mixing top-notch electronic sounds with distinctive guitar riffs, 'Passionate Reply' recalls the Foxx lyric approach, mixed effectively with the new Ultravox cutting-edge blend. Ure gives what could've been a throwaway effort a thorough vocal workout.

'Herr X' (Cann, Cross, Currie, Ure) 5:49

This German version of 'Mr. X' appeared alongside 'Passionate Reply' on the B-side of the 'Vienna' 12" single. This novelty version was the idea of Warren Cann (who was the voice on both versions) during recording, feeling it could be a B-side down the line. Though he knew some German, Cann had to enlist the help of Conny Plank's wife Krista in translating, with the producer serving as pronunciation coach during recording. Kraftwerk had undertaken the entirely opposite journey from German to English for *The Man-Machine*. The instrumental track is identical to 'Mr. X'.

'Alles Klar' (Cann, Cross, Currie, Ure) 4:53

Released as the B-side to 'All Stood Still', the title of this instrumental (except for Warren Cann's heavy breathing) was the result of a band in-joke. Having spent considerable time at Conny Plank's studio, the band had been surrounded by German-speaking staff. The phrase 'klar' and 'alles klar' – meaning 'That's all clear' or 'Yes, I understand' was often heard in discussions about the recording process. Cann executed the halting breath sounds in real time for over five minutes, noting wryly that today that'd be done once or twice, then sampled and used where needed. He admitted, 'By the end of the song, I nearly hyperventilated'.

'Face To Face' (Live) (Cann, Cross, Currie, Ure) 6:04

The 'Passing Strangers' B-side was from a concert at St. Albans City Hall on 16 August 1980. The song was never recorded in the studio. However, the 2020 40th-anniversary deluxe *Vienna* edition included two studio cassette recordings (one an instrumental) of a track titled 'Sound On Sound', which proved to be an early version of 'Face To Face'. The cassette version is stronger on the electronic components.

Some early press advertisements for the 'Passing Strangers' 7" listed 'Sound On Sound' as the B-side, and on some occasions in concert, Midge Ure introduced 'Face To Face' as 'Sound On Sound'. The song has strong echoes of 'All Stood Still' ('The system's gone' versus 'The system choked up'), which may be why it didn't make the album. It also has the opposite sentiments to 'Passing Strangers', which claims 'Quickly passes, time goes/ Time goes by too soon', while 'Face To Face' says there's 'Nothing but time, time/Time is all we had'.

There's much that connects this track to the Foxx era, which might've been another factor in its side-lining. The lyric changes 'Face to face/Room to room' into 'Sound on sound/Reel to reel', which maybe makes more sense, and again echoes the 'All Stood Still' line 'Tapes you might leave behind'. It seems the band were playing with themes across several tracks on what became *Vienna*, but 'Face To Face' never really found a secure niche. Warren Cann noted in Jonas Warstad's online interview, 'It just never came together properly'.

'King's Lead Hat' (Live) (Eno) 4:06

A live cover of the 1977 Brian Eno single from his album *Before And After Science*, the title famously being an anagram of Talking Heads, who Eno later produced.

This version – played live at London's Lyceum on 17 August 1980 – is a punky throwback that was never going to find a place on *Vienna*, but alongside 'Face To Face', was a B-side on the 'Passing Strangers' 12".

'Keep Talking' (Cann, Cross, Currie, Ure) 6:23

This 'All Stood Still' 12" B-side (alongside 'Alles Klar') was from a jam session when rehearsing for *Vienna*. The band found some sounds they wanted to develop further, including – according to Cann – 'a strange synth noise that seemed to sound vaguely like someone speaking'. The cassette recording was later released on the 40th anniversary *Vienna* edition. When Chrysalis pressured the band over the phone to give the track a title, someone said they'd 'keep talking' about it, when another pounced and declared, 'That's the title!'. The original B-side title was 'Keep Torq(u)e-ing' – a band in-joke, as, at one point, *Vienna* had the title *Torque Point*. Some elements were later explored in 'I Never Wanted To Begin', the B-side to 'The Thin Wall' from *Rage In Eden*.

'Animals' (Cann, Cross, Currie, Ure) 4:10

A surprise to most Ultravox fans, this track appeared in the 40th-anniversary edition as one of the cassette rehearsals that had been locked in the vaults since 1980. Almost fully formed, it wasn't a demo but a fully-fledged recording from the band's heyday. Opening with some studio chatter (Ure's voice can be heard), the track springs into life. It clearly didn't have a place on *Vienna,* but it could've been a decent B-side. It sounds like something Rich Kids or even Slik might've recorded, suggesting it was possibly an old Ure idea. It's a rough recording, and some vocals are indistinct, but its surfacing showed that Ultravox could still surprise their fans.

Rage In Eden (1981)

Personnel:
Midge Ure: lead vocals (except on 'Paths And Angles'), guitar, synthesizers
Warren Cann: drums, electronic percussion, backing vocals, lead vocals ('Paths And Angles')
Billy Currie: violin, viola, piano, synthesizers
Chris Cross: bass, synthesizers, backing vocals, guitar ('Paths And Angles')
Producer: Conny Plank
Recorded at Conny Plank's Studio, Cologne, West Germany
Label: Chrysalis
Release date: 11 September 1981 (UK)
Charts: UK: 4, US: 144, AUS: 20, CAN: 45, GER: 48, NL: 25, NZ: 4, NOR: 20, SW: 5
Running time: 45:34

The success of *Vienna* was a far cry from the John Foxx days when the public had ignored the band while they were appreciated by a certain wing of the music cognoscenti. Island Records repackaged selected tracks from their three Ultravox albums on the June 1980 compilation *Three-Into-One*, but it didn't trouble the album charts. A speculative re-release of the Foxx-fronted 'Slow Motion' made it to 33 in the UK in March 1981. Foxx was enjoying his own success as a solo artist, his debut *Metamatic* (including the Ultravox song 'Touch And Go' (a close relative of 'Mr. X')) reaching number 18 in February 1980, while the follow-up *The Garden* hit 24 in October 1981. Foxx also rode the Gary Numan electropop wave to some success with 'Underpass' (number 31), 'No One Driving' (32) and 'Burning Car' (35), though this was nowhere near the success of his former bandmates.

The problem was what to do next. Though *Rage In Eden* was to be the fifth Ultravox album, for Midge Ure and the *new* band, it was their tricky second album. The temptation – and public expectation – was to simply reproduce *Vienna*. They'd been on tour playing those songs in the autumn of 1981, so they were keen to progress their sound. Chris Cross told the TV show *Countdown* in 1981: 'We were always a little bit out of time with everything else that was going on. We decided to always maintain our own way the whole time'. According to Midge Ure, 'The idea of combining electronics with traditional rock instruments and classical instruments to make this noise that nobody else was making was fantastic'. To continue pushing themselves, they again turned to Conny Plank, setting up in his studio near Cologne in early 1981. Warren Cann told electrogarden.com:

For *Rage,* we didn't prepare anything. Roughly, we spent about a month doing all the loony things we'd always wanted to do in a studio, then a month coalescing it all into songs, and then about a month or so trying to wrangle mixes out of it – nearly drove us mad. Or perhaps that was just spending so much time out at Conny Plank's studio in the German countryside. It was the hardest record we'd ever made. We were extremely proud of the finished result. We did decide, however, not to go down that particular avenue again in a hurry. The merits of pure spur-of-the-moment inspiration aside, having at least a framework of material to flesh out once in the actual studio was something we were more comfortable with.

Midge Ure told superdeluxeedition.com that *Rage In Eden* was 'a brave record to do, and along with *Brilliant*, it's probably my favourite Ultravox album. With *Vienna*, we'd toured most of its songs before going into the studio, so it was incredibly quick to record. That was only three weeks. *Rage In Eden* was three months ... For most of the band, *Rage In Eden* was their fifth album, but it was only my second in Ultravox, so it could've easily been my difficult second album. Most people expected *Vienna* part two, but we didn't want that. We went off to Conny Plank's studio in the middle of nowhere outside Cologne with no ideas. We might've had a riff or a chord change, but we had zero songs, and we created the entire album in the studio. Conny's studio and his creativity became an instrument. We were either incredibly brave or incredibly naïve and stupid, but it turned out very well. We made an album we couldn't have made under any other circumstances'.

The result was a musically complex and more lyrically introspective album, devoid of obvious hit singles, with the exception of only two possibly valid tracks: 'The Voice' and 'The Thin Wall'. *Rage In Eden* approaches becoming a kind of electronic prog-rock concept album, with the tracks thematically and musically related. In fact, the final three tracks cross-fade, forming one long sequence. It was quite a difference from the distinct tracks that made up *Vienna*. Moving in this direction, the band were taking quite a risk. The result was the overall best Ultravox album.

One element they determined to control and carry forward from *Vienna* was the look of the album sleeves, which was put in the hands of designer Peter Saville (best known for his work with Factory Records and Joy Division). Cross noticed the similarity between the design work on *Vienna* and Joy Division's *Closer*. Ure described the band's partnership with Saville as 'a match made in heaven ... We were slow making the record, and Peter was even slower making the artwork'.

The main cover image idea of a face stylised with a single eye came from the work of French designer and illustrator Hervé Morvan (died 1980, aged 63), best known for a 1950s advertising campaign for Perrier. The original image – designed sometime in the 1930s – promoted Cinemonde (world cinema) with the slogan 'Visage du cinema mondial' (Face of world cinema) underneath. It's a striking image appropriated by Saville as the basis for the *Rage In Eden* cover, where it is no less striking. However, the initial usage was unauthorised, and after being faced with a lawsuit from the Morvan family, the cover was changed in subsequent reissues. By the time of the expanded 2008 *Rage In Eden* CD re-release, the issues had been satisfactorily resolved, allowing the use of the original, dramatic Peter Saville design once again, which was then carried over to the 40th Anniversary Deluxe Edition. (It was also used on the cover of the 2009 reunion concert CD/DVD *Return To Eden*). The mid-20th-century futurism of Ultravox's music and style had found the ideal expression in Saville's *Rage In Eden* design.

Rage In Eden spent 23 weeks in the UK album chart, peaking at number four. With sales of over 100,000, it was awarded gold disc status. As with *Vienna*, the press reaction was mixed. *Sounds* were fairly positive, declaring, 'The promise of *Vienna* is delivered', yet they worried that the band 'seem to take themselves too seriously'. *ZigZag* was more reserved: 'This album is Ultravox shine and glory, with hints of busting out'. For *Record Mirror*, the album was 'tepid in the extreme' with 'a complete lack of ideas'. *Melody Maker* thought Ultravox were taking cues from one of their imitators: 'It sounds like mature, devilishly clever Duran Duran – lush arrangements; obtuse, absurd lyrics'. Yet, the magazine noted the LP's 'confirmation, consolidation and class'.

In a retrospective review at allmusic.com, Dave Thompson wrote: 'Propulsive numbers like 'We Stand Alone' and 'I Remember (Death In The Afternoon)', the rebellious angst of 'Accent On Youth', the exotic strains of 'Stranger Within' and the haunting 'Your Name (Has Slipped My Mind Again)' all contained their own power. And even if the instrumental 'The Ascent' harkened back to 'Vienna', it was obvious that with *Eden*, Ultravox were climbing to grand new heights'.

Reviewing the 40th-anniversary edition, godisinthetvzine.co.uk awarded the album nine out of ten, declaring it an album of 'standouts ... the songs on *Rage In Eden* are almost prog at times, but they're never inaccessible. Both singles – 'The Voice' and especially 'The Thin Wall' were just commercial enough to break into the UK top 20 ... It's gloriously ominous-sounding, but at the same time, it's weirdly uplifting and invigorating ... *Rage In Eden* truly is their masterpiece, and the band know it'.

'The Voice' (Cann, Cross, Currie, Ure) 6:01

The album's second single was released on 29 October 1981. It's one of a selection of Ure-era tracks focused on singing, songs or dancing – key subjects that occupied the Blitz-era New Romantics, which Ultravox found themselves uncomfortably associated with. (For Ure, Visage was much more 'the house band of the Blitz club', especially as the project featured frontman Steve Strange.) Other tracks with similar dancing/singing themes include 'Serenade', 'Hymn', 'We Came To Dance' and 'The Song (We Go)' from *Quartet*, and 'Dancing With Tears In My Eyes' and 'Lament' from *Lament*.

As a sign of the group's evolution from *Vienna*, 'The Voice' was a strong choice to open *Rage In Eden* and had a radio-friendly pop feel. Ure delivers a classic, lively and delightful vocal, with the song and instrumentation playing to his strengths. It's a shame the single didn't crack the top ten but only climbed for five weeks, stalling at a reasonable 16 in November 1981, sticking around for a full 12 weeks.

There were two videos. Following the political concerns of earlier single 'The Thin Wall', 'The Voice' video (helmed by Russell Mulcahy, for the final time) focused on the media and its connection with politics and the law. Opening in a 1930s-style radio studio (with a dapper Billy Currie reading the news, accompanied by the huge text caption 'Wireless'), the video followed Warren Cann's journalist figure from a smoky bar to his typewriter ('The Press'), cutting to 'The People' who are *en masse* lapping-up the details of a 'big trial' (as the headlines blare), with a sweaty Ure in the dock. As 'The Law' sends Ure down, the focus switches to 'Command', as the video unreels images of war and conflict, connecting parental authority to that of commanding officers in the field. As white-clad divine or angelic figures unleash doves, the previous themes are connected in the guise of 'Television', upon which Currie tickles the ivories before everything comes together as 'The Voice'. It's a clever clip, dramatic and moody, and if nothing else, proves what up-for-anything hams the Ultravox band members were at their height.

The second video (made for German TV pop show *Bananas*) is a slightly more restrained performance piece, with the band playing the song in a strangely off-kilter 1950s-style living room. Fans fondly refer to this video as 'the wonky one'. The performance sections, against red curtains, feature two uncomfortable-looking women sitting centre-stage on a Salvador-Dalí-Mae-West-lips-type sofa.

'The Voice' is probably the album's most upbeat track, and it's surprising it wasn't the first single. Like much of the album, 'The Voice' has lush layers from programmed and live drums, throbbing bass work and Currie's ARP synthesizer. (He soon switched from analogue equipment to digital, losing something in the process.) This music set to Mulcahy's storytelling video, made for a perfect combination: the ideal fusion of a traditional rock 'n' roll band with the new 1980s technology.

The 'work in progress' version on the 40th-anniversary edition is more reserved and sounds slightly off compared with the finished item. Nonetheless, it's an interesting listen, revealing something of the band's work process as they strived for their unmistakeably unique sound.

'We Stand Alone' (Cann, Cross, Currie, Ure) 5:39

By far the single greatest Ultravox song, 'We Stand Alone' combines everything the band was capable of in one near-perfect track. It's a shame this wasn't considered viable as a single, as it may have performed better than the catchy 'The Thin Wall' or the anthemic 'The Voice'. It's a symphonic epic with lyrics that, for once, make perfect sense (mostly). It owes something to 'New Europeans' (great guitar work) and the emotions of 'Passing Strangers', shot-through with the melancholy that dominates *Rage In Eden*. This was indeed a band that had 'a different frame around us now' as a result of their success and fame with *Vienna*. It's a moody, high-toned track, which might've prevented it from being chosen as a single, but it worked very well when played live.

The title 'We Stand Alone' was an anthem for the band, an indication of their standing apart from mainstream early-1980s British pop and the cliched New Romantic movement. Though tarred with the New Romantic brush, Ultravox always did their own thing. Everything they achieved was due to their unique talents. With 'We Stand Alone', Ultravox produced a perfect pop song that was unfortunately not celebrated in its own right for its undoubted uniqueness.

'Rage In Eden' (Cann, Cross, Currie, Ure) 4:12

Built from glistening atmospheres, the title track is a piece of obscure mood music that's difficult to decipher. It's the ultimate in Ultravox indulgence and one of their best tracks. To some, it's slow and ponderous; to others, it's an attempt to create another 'Vienna'. (The return to prominence of the Roland CR-78 reinforces that idea.) The enigmatic backing vocals that fans have struggled to make out for decades are the chorus from the following track 'I Remember (Death In The Afternoon)' reversed! It's as if a time warp has somehow dragged elements of the next song back in time to feature – distorted – in this one. Warren Cann recalled to *Classic Pop* magazine: 'We used the studio fully as an instrument to make *Rage In Eden*. One day, we were working on 'I Remember (Death In The Afternoon)', and during the course of doing something backwards, we heard some backing vocals for the chorus in reverse. Backwards it sounded fantastic, like another language or a chant or whatever. It gave us an idea – we copied the backwards sound to a fresh reel of multitrack running the right way. From there, we built up the song 'Rage In Eden''.

There are few words here to make sense of – simply atmospheric sounds piled upon atmospheric sounds. Underpinned by a relentless programmed drum rhythm and packed with burbles and thrumming sounds, the track finally collapses in on itself as the sound switches to a ghostly mis-tuned radio overwhelmed by static and interference before a solid click, as if from an off switch, starts the next track. For Midge Ure, the song was a result of the band's self-consciously experimental approach to creating the album: 'The whole record was a malleable, ever-growing thing. We didn't make it one song at a time and onto the next one. We'd have songs in various degrees of development, going back in to say: 'Let's do this lyrical angle' or 'Why not try recording that backwards?'. It wasn't writing a bunch of songs around the piano and recording them in a linear fashion – it was jigsaw pieces done piecemeal. We pulled and pushed the ideas, knowing instinctively when to stop'.

As for the song's meaning, there are many interpretations. One subscribes to the 'alien astronaut' theory that advanced alien beings visited mankind in its infancy (Eden) and may even have helped in its development, possibly violently (Rage), as seen in Stanley Kubrick's *2001: A Space Odyssey*. That hinges on the couplet 'And they were the new gods/And they shone on high' combined with the opening line 'We sit and watch these lifeless forms/Stark and petrified'. It's also the kind of scenario realised in the opening sequence to Ridley Scott's 2012 *Alien* follow-up *Prometheus*. At the heart of the song is the hypnotic slow chorus '...focus on the main facade/Rage in Eden jigsaw sequence/But no one could see the end'. For some, the song is simply too slow and monotonous to be a strong entry in the canon, yet to others, it's the heart of the album – Ultravox's attempt at a concept album, with no clear or easily discerned concept at its centre. Cleverly, interpretation was best left to the individual listener.

'I Remember (Death In The Afternoon)' (Cann, Cross, Currie, Ure) 4:57

As 'Rage In Eden' clicks off, this powers in, with Currie's strings immediately demanding attention. The lyric follows on from the radio static: 'We turned the dial'. The song is clearly about premature death, about a group of friends losing someone (presumably famous, if their death was announced on the radio) close to them, then indulging in reminiscence of 'times we used to have'. A contemporary event – the unexpected death of John Lennon in December 1980 – comes to mind, especially in that awkward or shocked laughter at the news.

While the story (such as it is) matches the title, the title seems drawn from Ernest Hemingway's 1932 non-fiction book about Spanish bullfighting: *Death In The Afternoon*. Celebrating the rituals around bullfighting, it contemplates matters of time, memory, fear and courage, dealing with old men recalling their glory days of sports participation.

This hypnotic mood piece builds to an overwhelming crescendo, intertwining solos and arpeggios, then fading to close side one in fantastic, fatalistic style.

'The Thin Wall' (Cann, Cross, Currie, Ure) 5:39

Released as a single on 14 August 1981, this was the other track that had potential as a single (except perhaps for 'We Stand Alone'), a fact that may have proved to be a problem for Chrysalis. Driven by relentless electronic percussion (augmented by live drums) and built on sequences and a lively, urgent vocal, 'The Thin Wall' was the first of seven singles that made the charts but failed to crack the top ten. Billy Currie plays another violin solo, harsher than most, so befitting the almost threatening nature of the overall package. The choice of singles was left to the band. As Ure stated: 'Chrysalis never interfered. They never suggested, 'Where's the single?' or 'Here's your artwork and here's your latest video that we just need to stick you in somewhere'. All of that was left to us, so we worked with Peter Saville on the artwork, and *we* delivered the videos. That was a very unusual scenario'.

As with the album sleeve, Peter Saville Associates produced distinctive packaging for 'The Thin Wall', with black-and-white photography of disembodied arms emerging through a wall (an image seen in such films as Jean Cocteau's *La Belle et la Bête* and Roman Polanski's *Repulsion*), set against the band name and song title printed in gold. It certainly stood out when on display in record shops. Russell Mulcahy again directed the video, which showed the other band members seemingly pursuing Ure through a nightmarishly surreal funhouse. Ure is confronted with a deadly ceiling fan, a wonky chequerboard floor and the prospect of drowning in a flooded car. There are surreal images throughout, from those disembodied grabbing hands, swimmers half submerged in sand, and a glass (or ice) hand. There's a dash of film-noir style (a scene set at Rabat train station) and a suggestion of political plotting with an authoritarian edge, all seemingly revolving around the possession of a mysterious gold sphere that can be held in one hand.

What does it all mean? Well, the lyrics are not entirely helpful, adopting the William Burroughs' cut-up technique to generate lines – something John Foxx had practised, as did David Bowie before him. Ure noted: 'There was a lot of cut-and-paste Bowie-esque lyrics so that each line was like a soundbite from a movie or a book. The songs didn't necessarily have to tell a story; it was about a song giving you an overall image, a picture of what it was about'. Lines like 'Grey men who speak of victory/Shed light upon their stolen life' and 'Their velvet voices smooth and cold/Their power games a game no more/And long the chance to use it' suggest a paranoia about politics and those who wield power. The 'backs against the wall' image – as in a revolution – is suggested by the chorus lines, 'And those who know/ Will always feel their backs against the thin wall'. Film titles are also an inspiration: the line 'They drive by night' is the title of a 1940 Humphrey Bogart movie. However, the band have never lived down the bizarre line 'They shuffle with a bovine grace'.

Ure noted: 'This was at a time when music was allowed to be experimental, where you could play around and still have a chance of getting on the radio'. While radio airplay and hitting the higher reaches of the chart would be welcome, it was never the overriding aim, according to Cann (talking to Mike O'Connor at www.aylesburyfriars.co.uk): 'As for the commerciality of what we were doing, I can assure you that the very last thing on our minds was setting out to deliberately write commercial music. We always followed where the song wanted to go, irrespective of whether that was radio-friendly'. As it was, 'The Thin Wall' peaked at 14 in August 1981, spending eight weeks in the chart and seven in the top 40.

'Stranger Within' (Cann, Cross, Currie, Ure) 7:26
The first of four songs covering youth to old age, 'Stranger Within' deals with adolescence: a subject that several Foxx-era songs also tackled. This epic has echoes of 'Mr. X' in its almost-spoken components and rhythmic structure. The agonies of adolescence are clearly captured in the lyric's fear and anxiety about a time of mental and physical change.

Ure's agonised, echoed vocal adds to the throbbing, oppressive atmosphere conjured up in Cross's ominous bass line. The pulsing syncopation and pumping guitar and keyboard parts push the trajectory to its ultimately upbeat conclusion, but it's a struggle getting there. The haunting backing vocal, 'Don't fear the stranger within', grounds the teen agonies the singer is going through. Everyone extends their contributions, playing out the full potential of the noisy layers that build one upon another. Towards the end, the guitars even begin to sound like screeching birds: just one among many threatening sounds employed here. The bass part 'pops', just as the consolidation of the new, adult personality is achieved. It's a chrysalis-to-butterfly situation fraught with fears and dangers, none of which matter once the moment has passed.

A critic at postpunkmonk.com described 'Stranger Within' as 'the soundtrack to an atmospheric horror film'. Looked at from that angle, the transformation described (usually interpreted as adolescence) could equally be seen as a man-into-werewolf transformation!

'Accent On Youth' (Cann, Cross, Currie, Ure) 5:57

A sequel of sorts to 'Stranger Within', the title 'Accent On Youth' is more obvious from the lyric: 'What is this phase that I am going through?/Oh these precious years'. It's another tale of adolescence, but a somewhat clearer and more hopeful one than the previous track. Here we have the shedding of 'young depressive tears' and screams of 'frustration and lost control' that mark those teen years, with the reverberating backing vocal and chorus lines declaring 'Accent on youth/Attention/Ascends on you'. The song climaxes with the transformation from youth to adult completed: 'Let this man alone'.

Old movie titles come into play, *Accent On Youth* being a 1935 film about a young secretary's affair with her boss – a middle-aged playwright – further complicated when her boss's son falls for her. The phrase was also an episode title for *Kraft Theatre* in 1950 and was the name of a 1958 Australian version of *Top Of The Pops,* where new records were played to the delight of dancing teenagers.

This is a return to a more conventional song structure absent from much of the album. In an upbeat major key, 'Accent On Youth' follows the traditional verse/chorus/bridge construction. As a result, it's an uplifting listening experience after the angst that came before, even if the song itself is again about coming to terms with growing up. The serious lyrics are wrapped up in a positive-sounding musical confection.

'The Ascent' (Cann, Cross, Currie, Ure) 1:10

Essentially an instrumental extension of 'Accent On Youth', the two tracks run to over seven minutes before running into the final track. There is no instrumental to rival 'Astradyne' on *Rage In Eden*, as many tracks have extended instrumental breaks. The intense drums and percussion sound effects – including a fizzy top note – carry on through, the rest of the instrumentation falling away, building slowly to unleash Currie's viola solo. No one else sounded like this in 1981; no one even tried. The track climaxes with a piano flourish before crashing into the final track. Simply exquisite.

'Your Name (Has Slipped My Mind Again)' (Cann, Cross, Currie, Ure)
From youth to the other end of the age spectrum: old age, the effects of dementia, or a loss of awareness. Sparse instrumentation plays throughout while thundering drum crashes dominate. It's a slow track, with Ure's questioning vocal competing with that thumping percussion. Treated harmonies also run through the choruses. The lyric appears to describe a sensory loss mixed with random recollection ('I remember...'). Nothing is clear, either in vision or sound, for the song's narrator is trapped in a decaying body and tortured by a decaying mind ('A flashback image in my mind'). Slurred speech marks days that drag, while friends are lost either to death or simply recollection. The vocal seems to slip away as the life force diminishes. Is this song attempting to capture the actual moment of death? It's dark stuff for a supposed *pop* album, but that doesn't seem to have concerned the band, as Ure noted:

> You couldn't sit at the piano and write 'Your Name (Has Slipped My Mind Again)'. We couldn't see the final picture while we were making (*Rage In Eden*), but we could see that an interesting picture was coming together. When it was finished, we were all happy with it. It's a great example of a band working well together ... It's only later when you play it as an album and when you see people's reactions, that you think, 'Hold on, that's quite dark and intense'.

'Dark and intense' certainly captures the overall tone of *Rage In Eden* – the product of a band at the height of their powers, secure in the knowledge that the huge success of *Vienna* (album and single) gave them some leeway to do whatever they liked. It was an opportunity they didn't want to miss, and the result is a brooding, intense album that plays best as a whole. Side one is near perfect, with four great tracks, while side two plays out as an almost 15-minute symphony of despair and hope, ending in... death? Ure concluded: 'It was a combination of naivety and cockiness to think it was perfectly acceptable to go into the studio with nothing. We knew we had three months to make it, though if we'd known what that would cost, we might've tried to do it in one month. But it was a great way to do it. I've never spent that amount of time on one project before or since, and it was great to do'.

Related Tracks
'I Never Wanted To Begin' (Cann, Cross, Currie, Ure) 3:31
The marvellous B-side for 'The Thin Wall' was strong enough that it could've made it onto the album if the song sequence hadn't been so rigorously

controlled and programmed. Rhythmically, it's a good partner for the A-side. Everything works in conjunction, with the keyboards and drums given equal status and space. The chorus chant 'Name that sin' gives the song solid structure, but it's the rhythms that eventually dominate.

The lyric word salad is impenetrable, however. Just what does 'Shattered captives climbing gates to hold new lamps of fame/For mad kings rowing over lakes/Connecting rooms in black sedans' actually mean? The extended 12" version (6:17) gives the track room to breathe and escape from the lyric straightjacket and for Currie, in particular, to strut his stuff in an extended instrumental. There's maybe a hint of Orchestral Manoeuvres in the Dark here, especially in Ure's clipped vocal, but there's more than enough of the dark and moody trademark sound to make it distinctive.

'Paths And Angles' (Cann, Cross, Currie, Ure) 4:19
The B-side of 'The Voice' gave Cross an opportunity to try his hand at singing (in the chorus and fade). A lighter track than most on the album (in many ways anticipating some of the sounds on the following LP *Quartet*), 'Paths And Angles' nonetheless falls in line with much of the rhythmically driven *Rage In Eden* sound. Cann's vocal adopts the same almost spoken-word approach as on 'Mr. X'. In the middle, there's an epic Currie viola solo, playing gloriously against the almost monotonous programmed rhythm.

Cann, Currie, and Cross originated and recorded the track during the autumn 1981 UK tour while Ure was otherwise engaged. Though everything by the band was credited to all four, it's a fair bet that Cann wrote this lyric. Clinical, almost cold, the song seems concerned with images, visions, eyes and recording: the obsessions that touched many of the group's songs. The track seems to draw on celluloid motifs, citing film characters: 'with memories and faces', 'Some have values and decades of crime'. The entire thing ultimately dissolves into a lament (by Cross) for a 'lost camera' – a ghostly phrase that repeats until the fade, as if pining for a simpler time when film images were more iconic and meaningful than in that more modern era.

The band produced this track themselves, quite separate from the Conny Plank sessions – which helps explain the cleaner, less-layered sound. It looked forward to what the band would do next.

'Untitled I' (Cassette rehearsal) (Cann, Cross, Currie, Ure) 1:59
An instrumental draft of an unrealised song that was released as part of the 40th-anniversary edition, this has the basic elements but lacks the refinement the band ultimately applied to their best works. The drums are rudimentary, while the guitar part is a bit more developed, with a keyboard overlay that appears to be going somewhere. At just under two minutes, it's a live-in-the-studio doodle that shows some potential. It languished in the Chrysalis archives for the better part of four decades until it was unearthed and served up as a curiosity to sate endless fan interest.

'Untitled II' (Cassette rehearsal) (Cann, Cross, Currie, Ure) 2:50
An instrumental draft released in the 40th-anniversary edition, this curio shows the band playing with rhythm and percussion effects against some noodling keyboard and guitar lines. It reveals their working process for *Rage In Eden*. Cann's effective drumming is to the fore this time, with some 'Vienna' soundalike effects. The track runs out of steam eventually, ending with an almost-American railroad sound. Clearly, it wasn't something that they felt could ultimately make the grade, but it's a curious listen nonetheless.

'Paths And Angles'/'The Thin Wall' (Cassette rehearsal) (Cann, Cross, Currie, Ure) 5:28
This is an early version of 'Paths And Angles' that shows little of the finished track. However, it suggests the basic melody was in Currie's head before the song was ultimately recorded. The piano part morphs into an equally early take on elements that were to appear in 'The Thin Wall'.

Released in the 40th-anniversary edition, these tracks show how the musicians could disassemble speculative works and rearrange them in new ways to create entirely new tracks.

Quartet (1982)

Personnel:
Midge Ure: lead vocals, guitars
Warren Cann: drums, electronic percussion, backing vocals
Billy Currie: violin, keyboards
Chris Cross: bass, synthesizers, backing vocals
Producer: George Martin
Recorded at AIR Studios, London and Montserrat
Label: Chrysalis
Release date: 15 October 1982 (UK)
Charts: UK: 6, US: 61, AUS: 35, GER: 13, IRE: 10, NZ: 38, NOR: 19, JAP: 75,
SWE: 13
Running time: 40:54

Ultravox had been transformed by the addition of Midge Ure to the lineup. They'd gone from cerebral art rockers appreciated by the cognoscenti – but whose records didn't trouble the pop charts – to a hit-making machine with two top five albums in *Vienna* and *Rage In Eden*, and a string of hit singles, the most successful of which had been 'Vienna'. Every single from 'Vienna' to the final release from 1982's *Quartet* – 'We Came To Dance' – easily cracked the top 20. It was quite the turnaround in barely two years.

After the successful self-indulgence of *Rage In Eden*, Ultravox were determined to do things differently. For their third album with Ure (sixth overall), they moved on from entering the studio with no material, though it had been successful. For what became *Quartet*, they developed the songs in rehearsal long before booking expensive studio time. This had been the approach adopted prior to *Vienna*, though that album's material also had a thorough workout on tour before being recorded.

Over three months of intermittent work, they produced much material, but had trouble making it cohesive. Finally settling on eight individual songs (not thematically linked – so more like *Vienna* than *Rage In Eden*), they turned their attention to finding a new producer. Always looking to keep things fresh, they felt that after three albums with Conny Plank, it was time for a fresh set of ears. Ure claimed in 1983: 'It was getting a bit safe. We knew if we recorded with (Plank) again, it would be great and we'd be really happy ... but there would be no excitement'.

Their ultimate choice of producer came as a surprise to many, not least themselves – George Martin, the production mastermind behind The Beatles (he produced all Beatles albums except for *Let It Be*). This was an out-of-left-field choice – either the product of ambition (positive) or arrogance (negative). When the new Ultravox signed with Chrysalis (originally founded in 1969), one of the attractions was the label's US arm (active since 1976). If the band played their cards right, they might finally 'break' America. It was that possibility that attracted them to George Martin, who agreed to take on the job because his daughter Lucy was an avowed Ultravox fan. As Midge Ure said (suggesting their arrogance was at least self-aware), 'If Ultravox were ever going to listen to anybody, George Martin was the person'. Ure expanded on this in an interview with a German press agency: 'When it came to taking advice from others, Ultravox were difficult. There were few people we would've listened to. But Sir George Martin was one of them. When George tells you something, you listen'.

Quartet was recorded in two parts – the first in London's AIR Studios between June and July 1982, and the second at AIR's Caribbean outpost in Montserrat (a former British Overseas Territory) in July and August. Air was established by George Martin in 1979 as a purpose-built studio that recreated all the technical possibilities already available in his London original. The exotic location soon attracted many 1980s artists, including Dire Straits, The Police, Paul McCartney, Elton John, Duran Duran and Michael Jackson, among others. The studio closed down following the destruction wreaked by island-wide Hurricane Hogu in 1989. Many who'd recorded there – including Midge Ure – helped Martin in a fundraising drive to aid the island's rebuilding.

In an interview with the American Ultravox fan club magazine *The Voice*, Billy Currie recalled the process that led to *Quartet*:

We put all the tracks down in four weeks at Air Studios in Oxford Circus, which was quite frantic. I think George Martin did a lot on the vocals, but he also influenced us quite a bit on one or two of the musical arrangements. Then, when we went over to Montserrat, it was exactly the same mixing desk and speakers, but time to think about it and organise all this energy because there was a lot of energy on the tracks.

Talking to Michael Casano at *electrogarden.com* in 2002, Warren Cann expressed some disappointment at the results, though he'd enjoyed the process:

Our choice of working with George was another example of a great idea – certainly to us – which backfired and was totally misinterpreted by everyone else. We wanted to work with George Martin, the man who produced what is considered one of the greatest albums of all time: *Sgt. Pepper's Lonely Hearts Club Band*. We got slammed for working with *Mr. Mainstream*. We'd lost it and had 'sold out'. This was the guy whose work on that pioneering record has been assimilated by every band on the planet. When we approached him, we were well aware he'd been working with more conservative acts. We made it clear we weren't wallflowers in the studio ... We were game for anything. It didn't turn out quite as we'd imagined. Perhaps George was tired, or perhaps we were suffering from our own misconceptions, but it was a rather sedate experience and not the liberating sonic voyage we were expecting. However, I wouldn't trade that adventure for anything.

As usual, the music press were indifferent or actively hostile to the new work. *NME* laid out their take, plainly, reviewing the band rather than the album: 'Ultravox have perfected the art of taking the vacuous phrase and making it sound like profound philosophy ... They're too composed and self-conscious to seriously threaten emotional complacency, and too grandiose to be an elevating pop hope'. For *Sounds*, Ultravox were 'well-equipped to be making music that could enthral, inspire and seduce. Instead, they're stuck in a post-seduction phase of merely stroking a lover's forehead when a little more stimulation is required'. In *Melody Maker*, the take was that 'This gleaming music could dazzle even (producer) Trevor Horn ... Ultravox aim straight for the target. They score alright, but it is a triumph of expediency, and an easy victory is easily forgotten'. It's as if the critics found it difficult to engage with the music on its own terms.

That didn't stop fans and music lovers from buying into what the band were offering. *Quartet* had a longer run in the UK charts than *Rage In Eden* – a total of 30 weeks, with an opening peak in October 1982 at number six. It spent 19 weeks in the top 40, six in the top 20, and two in the top ten: enough to ensure another gold disc (for sales in excess of 100,000).

The band embarked upon their largest tour to date – the *Monument* tour – from November 1982 to May 1983, taking in shows in the UK/Europe, US, Canada and Japan. The support band were Messengers (Danny Mitchell and Colin King), who also sang backing vocals. The tour boasted a huge symbolic stage set in a bland grey colouring that only came to life when the stage lighting was applied. It proved to be something of a burden, as the complex set had to fit into many auditoriums.

The tour resulted in the six-track live album *Monument*, which reached nine in the UK and was certified gold. There was also a live video of the *Monument* album, running for 45 minutes. An extended and revised 2009 CD/DVD re-release had nine tracks in total. It was the band's only live album until 2010's *Return To Eden: Live At The Roundhouse,* which captured the band's triumphant reunion.

'Reap The Wild Wind' (Cann, Cross, Currie, Ure) 3:49
The opening track immediately reveals the new, cleaner sound the band were pursuing. Released as a single on 16 September 1982, it preceded the album, so was the first taste of the new direction. The song title was taken from the 1942 romantic adventure movie directed by Cecil B. DeMille and starring Ray Milland, John Wayne and Paulette Goddard.

In 2018, Ure explained their method of writing lyrics: 'We used the words and the voice as a rhythmic sound, almost like an instrument itself: a canvas of words. One line does not necessarily connect to the next. Take 'Reap The

The 1984 Ultravox lineup for *Lament* – a more hirsute band than ever before. (*Alamy*)

Left: The cover of the band's self-titled debut album *Ultravox!*, released in 1977 – a hybrid punk and 'art rock' effort. (*Island*)

Right: Also released in 1977, Ultravox's second album *Ha!-Ha!-Ha!* saw their sound develop in a new wave direction. (*Island*)

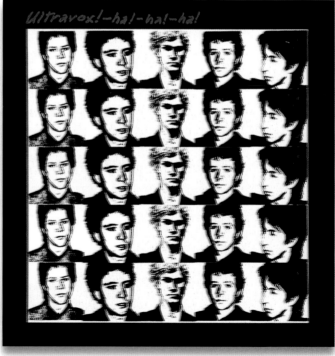

Right: The third John Foxx-fronted album, *Systems Of Romance*, displayed a new level of musical sophistication. (*Island*)

Left: Distinctive black and white photography and severe personal styling created the enduring Ultravox image from 1980. (*Chrysalis*)

Left: John Foxx leading Ultravox in an iconic performance *Live At The Rainbow* in 1977.

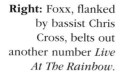

Right: Foxx, flanked by bassist Chris Cross, belts out another number *Live At The Rainbow*.

Left: Stevie Shears played guitar on the first two John Foxx Ultravox! albums.

Right: Billy Currie and his trademark violin – perhaps the true heart of classic eighties Ultravox.

Left: Midge Ure channels movie star Clark Gable with his moustache, sideburns, and loose bowtie on stage in the 1980s.

Right: Warren Cann hitting the skins during a 1980 concert in St Albans.

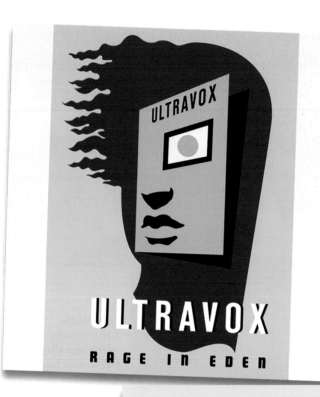

Left: The iconic original cover of *Rage In Eden* by Peter Saville draws on a 1930s design. (*Chrysalis*)

Right: An architectural approach was taken to the graphics for 1982's *Quartet*, produced by The Beatles' producer George Martin. (*Chrysalis*)

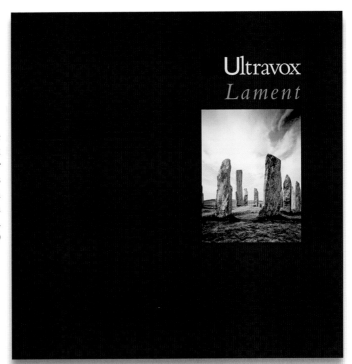

Right: The embossed 'black squares' cover for *Lament* features the Callanish standing stones on the Isle of Lewis. (*Chrysalis*)

Left: Known as 'the pink thing' and disliked by many fans, *U-Vox* was the final Ultravox album from the eighties. (*Chrysalis*)

Left: Midge Ure leads the chorus in 'The Voice' music video, the final one directed by Russell Mulcahy.

Right: 'The Thin Wall' video features imagery from films like *Beauty And The Beast* (1946) and *Repulsion* (1965).

Left: An example of Ultravox's unique approach to abstract images in music videos ('The Thin Wall').

Right: The eighties foursome in a still from the 'We Came To Dance' music video.

Left: Ultravox with The Chieftans collaborating on the overblown 'All Fall Down'.

Right: Billy Currie performing on 'All Fall Down', the final Ultravox hit single.

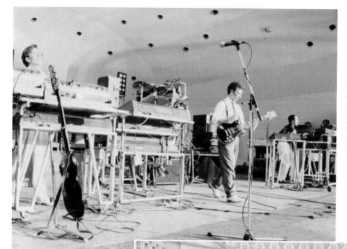

Left: The band playing *Vienna*-era tracks at the Crystal Palace Bowl 'Summer In The City' concert in June 1981. (*Getty*)

Right: At the height of their eighties fame, Ultravox regularly toured Europe, seen here in Paris in 1982. (*Getty*)

Left: Ultravox – minus drummer Warren Cann – launch the controversial *U-Vox* album at HMV in 1986. (*Shutterstock*)

Right: Midge Ure partnered with Bob Geldof in the Band Aid/Live Aid project, winning an Ivor Novello Award in 1984. (*Alamy*)

Left: Ultravox took a two-year break while Midge Ure worked on Band Aid, seen here at Gatwick Airport. (*Alamy*)

DRINKING WATER ONLY

LOVE BAND AID

Right: Midge Ure fronted Ultravox's performance at Wembley for Live Aid on 13 July 1985 in front of 72,000 people. (*Getty*)

Left: The minimalist cover for *Revelation*, the 1993 Ultravox revival attempted by Billy Currie. (*DSB*)

Right: The second nineties album, *Ingenuity*, took scientific progress as a theme. (*Intercord*)

Right: The unexpected 2012 album *Brilliant*, with a clever design suggesting the title is, in fact, a question rather than a boast ... (*Chrysalis*)

Left: Career retrospective *The Collection* was the band's biggest-selling album, reaching number two in the charts in November 1984. (*Chrysalis*)

Left: Producer Stephen Lipson and Midge Ure working on the *Brilliant* album, recorded between 2010 and 2011 around the world.

Right: Billy Currie and Midge Ure working on the *Brilliant* album.

Left: Chris Cross working on a keyboard part for *Brilliant* at Midge Ure's studio in Canada.

Right: In Autumn 2012, Ultravox toured the UK in support of *Brilliant*, mixing classic tracks with those from the final album.

Left: Midge Ure singing 'Rise', one of the cracking Ultravox tracks from *Brilliant*.

Right: Billy Currie indulging in one of his classic keyboard parts on stage in 2012.

Left: The cover for the belated 2022 release of the 1977 John Foxx-fronted concert *Live At The Rainbow*. (*UMC/Island*)

Right: The live *Monument* album was the only live Ultravox concert recording available during the eighties. (*Chrysalis*)

Left: The 1993 compilation album that mixed Midge Ure solo work with Ultravox and Visage hits. (*Chrysalis*)

Wild Wind': it's really not about anything at all! 'Reap The Wild Wind' is all about the melody and the rhythm of the song'. Ure expanded on this for the 2023 *Quartet* 40th-anniversary deluxe edition liner notes:

> It was written differently from anything we had written before and started off as an idea rather than as a song … It's a piece of music we came up with, and we thought we'd mix a strong melodic theme with lyrics that don't necessarily make any sense or tell a story, that doesn't have a traditional beginning, middle and end. Our theory was that a lot of our European or Japanese fans don't speak English as a first language and don't really understand what the songs are about. It was more about the sound of the words. Here, they blend well with the sound of the music. Everyone thought it was a strange song, but it worked.

Whatever it's about, the song certainly worked well enough to reach number 12 in the UK, spending nine weeks on the chart, with three of them in the top 20. It was also their first single to reach the US charts, a long-held ambition for the band. The song peaked in the *Billboard* Hot 100 at 71 on 9 April 1983, reaching 27 in the US rock chart on 26 March 1983. They were the highest points Ultravox would ever reach in the US – failing to make the significant, sustained breakthrough there that some of their contemporaries managed.

The song's video was the first directed by Midge Ure and Chris Cross, having taken on the responsibility from Russell Mulcahy. The result is a curious mix of aviator flyboy hi-jinks as the band play Spitfire pilots. The construction of an abstract monument was modelled after the Peter Saville graphics that appeared on the covers of the *Quartet* album and the 'Reap The Wild Wind' single. The monument motif continued through the *Monument* tour. The video ends with the completion of the monument, and the text scroll, 'This film is dedicated to those who gave their all … everywhere'. Ure and Cross were almost as interested in the band's developing visual side as they were the music and had learnt much from working with Mulcahy. Ure had already directed videos for Steve Strange and Visage: notably 'Visage' (shot at the Blitz club) and 'The Damned Don't Cry' (filmed at Tenterden Town Station, Kent). In notes for the deluxe edition, Ure recalled making the video: 'Reap The Wild Wind' was done at a little airstrip in Berkshire and at Beachy Head … I remember on the day, a gale was blowing in from the sea, which kind of suited the song! We could live out some fantasies, such as using a Spitfire, which was quite expensive to do'. The pair saw little need for the video to slavishly follow the lyrics. Ure said, 'You can put across a different aspect of the song, which doesn't have to be what the film is about. We could make it grand and strange-looking … we'd write music with images in our heads, but (making videos) was like doing it the other way around: making images for music'.

'Serenade' (Cann, Cross, Currie, Ure) 5:05

Second track 'Serenade' is a prime example of the band's tendency in this period to write about the nature of songs themselves, aspects of performance, dancing or pop music (See also 'Hymn', 'We Came To Dance' and 'The Song (We Go)' on *Quartet*; 'Dancing With Tears In My Eyes' and 'Lament' on *Lament*). A serenade is a performance given in honour of someone or something. They are typically calm, light pieces of music. The term comes from the Italian word *serenata*, which derives from the Latin *serenus*, meaning serenity.

The use of digital synthesizers is to the fore here (replacing their previous analogue kit), giving a cleaner, sharper sound and adhering to the emerging MIDI standards. The result was a lighter, less-layered sound, obvious from 'Serenade'. Each element here is pin-prick sharp (unlike many of the tracks on the delightfully murky *Rage In Eden*). As a result, the instrumental interludes can seem a little sparse. Backing everything up is the reliably chunky drumming from Cann and the solid vocal from Ure.

In the move from Conny Plank, Ultravox had lost some of their mystery in a bid for pop success. That may have been on their minds, hence phrases like 'rhythm and swing', 'hunted melodies' and 'the fable and the rhymes', although there is something uncomfortably authoritarian and populist in the couplet 'The chant of a thousand-fold/The song of a million strong'.

Apparently considered as a possible single, two variations of 'Serenade' were prepared: the 'Single version' and an extended 12" 'Special remix' (running to 6:01). The latter was featured on a bonus disc of six remixes accompanying two limited editions of the 1984 greatest hits package *The Collection* released in the UK, Australia and New Zealand. Like many of the Quartet tracks, 'Serenade' offers a more pop-focused sound which is simpler, drier and even thin compared to the triumphs of *Rage In Eden*. It's not necessarily worse, just different. It is evident that Ultravox sacrificed something ineffable in their pursuit of US pop success that was to remain so elusive.

'Mine For Life' (Cann, Cross, Currie, Ure) 4:44

Unlike the preceding tracks, 'Mine For Life' is an effective story song with a series of narrative vignettes building a larger picture where the lyrics are actually meaningful. There's noir imagery in the 'man with a suitcase' section (echoing 'Mr. X'), while those focused on the frustrated poet and the graffiti-writing youth suggest struggles with self-expression and creativity. Each character feels there must be more meaning or reward to be drawn from their pursuits, whether it be life, love or, indeed, hate.

The music is well-structured, with a wonderful instrumental break where Cross and Currie get to strut their stuff – Currie enjoying an extended (if rather underwhelming) synth part during the bridge – while the choral vocal backing that was so much a part of *Rage In Eden*, returns. Guitar (given the lead slot here) and drums are greatly to the fore, as in much of George

Martin's production, but the synths aren't relegated to the background but play a substantial role in the overall effect. This song was played slightly faster live, giving it fresh urgency and a stronger punk edge.

'Mine For Life' was included on the live album *Monument* derived from the 1982/1983 tour. Of the six tracks on the initial release, four were single releases ('Reap The Wild Wind', 'The Voice', 'Vienna' and 'Hymn'), with the 'Hymn' B-side 'Monument' used as an atmospheric intro. The only non-single was 'Mine For Life'. The instrumental 'monitor mix' on the anniversary edition is a more chunky version. 'Mine For Life' – which could've easily suited *Vienna* – remains a connoisseur favourite.

'Hymn' (Cann, Cross, Currie, Ure) 5:46
Released as a single on 2 November 1982, there was always something of Christmas attached to the atheistic 'Hymn'. It reached a high of 11 in the UK on 27 November, remaining in the chart for a phenomenal 11 weeks (eight in the top 20 and ten in the top 40), finally exiting the top 100 in early February 1983. Across the 1982 Christmas period and into 1983, 'Hymn' enjoyed exceptional radio airplay, partly attributable to its superficial suitability for the time of year.

The definition of a hymn as a devotional song written for adoration or prayer, typically addressed to a deity or deities, certainly fits these lyrics. In the anniversary edition liner notes, Ure looked back on the song's origin:

Billy came up with a hymn-like theme for the main melody. He played it on a very grand-sounding instrument, and we thought it was very Russian-esque because that's the area he was classically trained in. We started working around the theme, and the lyrics came quite quickly. We tended to get sections of the music right, the basis of the choruses, the verse and the middle sections, and then we'd go away and work on it and the lyrics and piece everything together like a jigsaw. We'd carry on changing it until we got something we were satisfied with.

Currie recalled that 'Hymn' came together very quickly in rehearsal: 'I remember 'Hymn' had a great vibe straight away, and a burst of energy which we'd lacked a little on *Rage In Eden*. There was more of a balance of electronics and live work, a change in producer in George Martin and engineer Geoff Emerick. We were really up for it and were in a good place'.

'Hymn' is something of a departure for Ultravox, though there may have been an intention to deliberately attempt a new 'Vienna'. Critic Dave Thompson at allmusic.com has suggested that the opening notes of the melody line were partially borrowed from Zones' 1979 song 'Mourning Star' from their album *Under Influence*. There may be a superficial resemblance, though Ultravox have never commented on it. Otherwise, the tracks are very different. Interestingly, Zones emerged from the ashes of Midge Ure's earlier band Slik. 'Mourning Star' was released in July 1979, but when the single and album failed to chart (despite support from Radio 1's John Peel), Zones split up. Given the connection, the vague similarity becomes more intriguing.

Currie came up with the basic melody and developed the bridge section, and the lyrics were a joint effort between Cann, Cross and Ure. Cann led the way, developing the chorus (the section that most resembles 'Mourning Star', oddly), while Cross and Ure focused on the verses. The song's meaning was reputedly driven by Cann's self-declared atheism. In fact, it goes one step further in outlining the potential corrupting elements of blind belief ('faithless in faith'), the self-centred interpretation of scripture ('Different words said in different ways/Have other meanings from he who says') and the true ambitions of many who declare their faith ('The power and the glory'), perhaps with particular relevance to the US's growing Christian evangelical movement in the 1980s. The source of religion (in the West largely the Bible) is dismissed as 'the storybook'. 'Hymn' may have sounded like a nice Christmas pop song, but scratch the surface and there's so much more to be mined.

'Hymn' was supported by a spectacular music video, again directed by Ure and Cross. The video picks up at a screening for the video from 'Reap The Wild Wind' (as seen on a cinema screen) and then follows Warren Cann leaving the cinema (London's The Screen on the Green; he pauses by a *Raiders Of The Lost Ark* poster – Steven Spielberg's 1981 Harrison Ford movie that later inspired the Ultravox video for 'Love's Great Adventure'), only to be tempted by a green-eyed demonic figure (played by Zürich-born actor Oliver Tobias, then perhaps best known for 1978's *The Stud*. Ure said: 'He was a neighbour of Rusty Egan's, and I'd often bump into him when seeing Rusty. We had managed to talk him into wearing these fluorescent contact lenses, which he couldn't get out at the end, which caused a bit of panic for both him and us!'). Cann signs a contract offering success as an international film star. Similar vignettes follow featuring the other band members – Currie plays a hopeless politician who signs his contract and wins power (for 'The People's Party', echoing the video for 'The Voice'); Ure is shown playing in a band, largely ignored by his audience, before signing his contract (at the venue's bar), resulting in him being introduced on *Top Of The Pops* by David Jensen (an experience Ure was actually all too familiar with). Cross is a lowly caterer serving the 'great and the good' in a company boardroom whose contract propels him from tea boy to the top of the corporate ladder. The four are then shown in a chequered-floor limbo where their souls have apparently been 'reaped' by Tobias' Devil, only for them to suffer the torments of the damned, reflecting their various ambitions. The final image is of the contract they all signed, burning up and flying away as embers. The work reflects and reinforces the song's abstract concerns and builds on the concise storytelling in sharp images that Russell Mulcahy pioneered with the video for 'The Voice'.

While the visual elements from the *Quartet* sleeve carried over into the 'Reap The Wild Wind' and 'Hymn' single covers, the latter – for some reason – also features Masonic imagery such as the compass and the square. However, rather than referring to Freemasonry or connecting it with the song's meaning, it simply appears to be Peter Saville's playful use of builders tools, as also featured in the monument building portions of the 'Reap The Wild Wind' video.

'Visions In Blue' (Cann, Cross, Currie, Ure) 4:38

This unexpectedly subdued opener of side two was also a perhaps surprising third single. Released on 11 March 1983, it reached 15 in the UK charts on 26 March and remained there for six weeks, four of them in the top 40. There's something of the 'Vienna' vibe about the slow opening and the prominent piano motif. That didn't connect with everyone, though, with *Smash Hits* reviewer David Hepworth writing, 'I blew the dust off the stylus, changed the turntable speed, and got the bloke in from next door to check my wiring. But no use. This still sounded awfully dirge-like'.

Certainly, it's a slow build, gradually adding elements (percussion, humming synth drones) right through to the moment the pace suddenly picks up at almost two minutes in. Crashing drums, Currie's violin solo, and synth support run through the track as Ure's vocal takes something of a back seat to the dramatic instrumentation. A minute from the end, it all crashes into silence, Ure wrapping up his vocal against the returning piano. It's a dramatic track that retreats from its crescendo only to elegantly fade away.

According to Ure, 'Visions In Blue' was 'another image-conscious song. There's a vague theme running through it, but it's a love song, as 'Vienna' was, but an off-the-wall love song. It's like a series of romantic images pieced together as if someone had cut lines from love letters and pieced them together to make an off-the-wall story'. That's supported by the lyric, mixing faces in windows with ashes of memories, portraits and pictures with oaths made in silence. There's a mysterious story here, but it's up to the listener to fully decode it. Whatever its meaning, 'Visions In Blue' failed to recreate the success of 'Vienna', partly due to limited airplay (Radio 1 playlists were becoming ever-more restrictive and solidly mainstream, so anything slightly unusual was relegated to late-evening shows like John Peel's) and perhaps the controversy over the video.

Directed once more by Cross and Ure, the broadcaster rated the original version of the video as too 'blue' to transmit – naked breasts were not about to get an airing on *Top Of The Pops*! The video opens with the monument graphic once more, this time carved into condensation on a frosted window. It then depicts two youthful women (straight out of a Jean Rollin Euro vampire movie) intercut with Ure performance footage (fittingly, a blue-lit disembodied face). Admittedly, there are lesbian undertones, with one scantily clad woman bathing the feet of a topless woman, but it's all essentially innocent enough, soft-core stuff. A brief horse ride later, we're into the dramatic, colourful ballroom sequence in which a woman dressed as a military man dances with a 1920s flapper type. It resembles something you might've seen down the Blitz club or even in a Ure-directed Visage video. The fact that we're watching two women dancing (not that well disguised) is revealed fully when one's breasts are exposed. Playing with identity – sexual or otherwise – was a favourite pastime of the New Romantics, and this video and all its tropes fitted right in with that movement. Quite why Cross and Ure thought they could get such imagery broadcast on BBC 1 at 7 pm during *Top Of The Pops* is an open question. The BBC and MTV both instituted outright bans on the video, thus limiting exposure for the song. If the aim was to boost sales by creating a controversy, it didn't really work. A family-friendly version of the video was ultimately created, which did finally get an airing on *Top Of The Pops* on 17 March 1983.

'When The Scream Subsides' (Cann, Cross, Currie, Ure) 4:17
The gentle fade-out from 'Visions In Blue' is met with this shock, cold opening as Cann belts out the backing vocal line 'And we talked' before Ure kicks in with 'Just the two of us'. Then it's off to the races. Is it a simple song about a casual romance?: 'Nothing serious/Time is on our side'. Or is it something much darker, a precursor to 'Dancing With Tears In My Eyes', an apocalyptic scenario?: 'Yes, we took the role of the lovers and the friends/ And we played the parts till the words came to an end'. The melancholy central section supports that, just preceding Currie's trademark pitch-bending synth line (one of the few on *Quartet* to actually have an impact).

It's short enough not to be self-indulgent, and – like many of the album tracks here – the song had great single potential. The call-and-response vocals easily recall something like 'All Stood Still', and *that* had proven to be a great counter-intuitive single choice.

'We Came To Dance' (Cann, Cross, Currie, Ure) 4:14
The fourth and final *Quartet* single (two more than from *Rage In Eden*: proving the single-friendly nature of the material here), 'We Came To Dance' was the last in a run of seven consecutive top 20 hits: a consistent run many bands from the time would've envied. Released on 23 May 1983 (some sources state 18 April), the single peaked at 18 on 28 June. It stuck around in the charts for seven weeks, five in the top 40.

Having moved away from the monument-inspired sleeve graphics ('Visions In Blue' had featured a red-to-blue colour chart and some interesting calligraphy), the 'We Came To Dance' sleeve boasted a graphic of a mountaintop. The drums and the melody make for a solid track (more 'Vienna' callbacks here), with Ure's vocal (verses against stark percussion) and minimum, subtle synth backing until the central spoken-word section from Cann: 'Take what you can, they said'. Cann's deep-voiced vocals often added something intangible to the overall Ultravox package, so it's great to see him given more prominence across *Quartet*, even though the album lacks a solo showcase for him.

Given the fuss that greeted the 'Visions In Blue' video, it seems that the 'We Came To Dance' clip has been all but forgotten. Showing the band visiting an exhibition of Chinese peasantry artwork that comes to life in live-action clips, it's abstract and somehow removed from the song. There's an on-the-run romance (which ends in suicide!) that plays out under the instrumental section (lacking Cann's spoken interlude, which is only on the album cut). Shot in a quarry with a substantial cast, it was no doubt expensive but feels somehow inconsequential. There's more storytelling ambition here, perhaps indicating a direction that Ure hoped to move in: 'Chris and I talked about making a feature film, something more visual than musical, but we never got our act together. During the Australian and Japanese leg of the tour, we filmed as we went around, with the idea of making a documentary, but again, we never got around to fully fleshing out the idea'.

'Cut And Run' (Cann, Cross, Currie, Ure) 4:18
If *Quartet* had ended with 'We Came To Dance' (maybe in an extended version), it might've rated higher in fans' collective opinions (although it might also have required at least one more additional track, perhaps one of the B-side instrumentals). As it is, the album closes with two of its weaker tracks. 'Cut And Run' at least benefits lyrically from another storytelling approach, which was something missing from most of the tracks. The film-noir elements (guns, knives, cigarettes) are all present, rolling out at a hectic pace. That's quickly broken with Currie's piano under Ure's vocal describing the trapped nature of a noir figure (detective, fugitive) who's been manipulated by the forces of fate into an impossible position ('And he tries to forget all that forces every move'). It's a solid enough track but somehow lacking. An alternative reading suggests a lovelorn suicide: 'One more twist of the knife and it's time to cut and run/Cries on his tape so they might understand/Signs his farewell with a squeeze of his hand'. If so, it's the album's second track (at least) to take that turn.

There's a musical echo (albeit much simplified) of this track on 'Something To Do' – the opening song on Depeche Mode's fourth album *Some Great Reward* (1984).

'The Song (We Go)' (Cann, Cross, Currie, Ure) 3:56
Little appreciated by fans, 'The Song (We Go)' at least gave the band the central drum break (through to the fade), which was repurposed to close 'The Voice' as a gig finale from 1983 onwards (all four band members violently thumping drum pads at the front of the stage), and that song has been performed live that way ever since. It certainly made for a rousing and unorthodox conclusion to an Ultravox gig. Otherwise, 'The Song (We Go)' is

an unfortunate closer (a B-side at best, as it's a musical doodle and nothing more). It's another song concerned with songs, referring to 'syncopated rhythms' and 'a hundred-thousand heartbeats'. It's lightweight, lacks content (although it's much better and heavier live, as on *Monument*), and was a bit of a lark if Ure is to be believed: 'George Martin insisted on not working Sundays and having time off from the studio, which was a little strange to us having worked seven days a week with Conny Plank. He was more than happy for us to go in and play around when he was not there'. It appears that 'The Song (We Go)' was the result of one of these unsupervised Sunday sessions when the kids were at play. Ure continued in the anniversary edition notes:

If I remember correctly, no engineer was present to run the desk, but we managed to bluster our way through the recording process in a very hit-or-miss way. We balanced Warren's Simmons electronic drum pads above the meters on the console and played them looking towards the faders where the producer/engineer would sit. The song was a jam based on the syncopated drum rhythms we loved from the likes of Neu! and La Düsseldorf, with a simplistic sing-along chorus anyone could join in with. I think we wanted something light and – dare I say – happy. I think that's what we got.

Related Tracks
'Hosanna (In Excelsis Deo)' (Cann, Cross, Currie, Ure) 4:21
An instrumental B-side to 'Reap The Wild Wind', 'Hosanna (In Excelsis Deo)' continues – in the title at least – the religiosity of 'Hymn'. In keeping with 'Hymn' and 'Serenade', a hosanna is either an appeal for divine help (in Judaism) or an expression of praise (in Christianity). The other part of the title comes from the Christian hymn 'Gloria in excelsis Deo' – meaning 'Glory to God in the highest', fitting with the Christian meaning of offering praise, as in 'Praise be to God'. It's a strange strain that runs through much of *Quartet* that is not particularly reflected in the lyrics themselves ('Hymn' being the notable exception, although atheist-inspired). It's not a particularly religious piece of music, but it is nicely atmospheric nonetheless, with a nice fretless bass (perhaps Cross was influenced by Mick Karn from the UK group Japan?) and a dominant synth line running throughout. This piece could've easily found a place on *Quartet* instead of 'Cut And Run' or 'The Song (We Go)' as an album instrumental in the style of 'Astradyne'.

It builds nicely to a climax (it could've easily run for another minute or so, perhaps matching 'Astradyne's seven minutes) and features some of the *Rage In Eden* layered atmospherics missing from much of *Quartet* – given the George Martin minimal approach to production, focusing on a frosty precision and clarity. Of Ultravox, Martin remarked in the *Monument* video: 'They are, without a doubt, the most musical group I've come across in recent years'.

'Monument' (Cann, Cross, Currie, Ure) 3:16

Released as the B-side to 'Hymn', the moody and almost-sinister 'Monument' was also used as the intro music for the 1982/1983 *Monument* tour and featured on the live album/video. Like the previous track, it's an atmospheric piece of pseudo-soundtrack music (perhaps suitable for a John Carpenter film), an experiment that could've developed into a full song if lyrics had been added. (The same applies to 'Hosanna (In Excelsis Deo)'.) The grandiosity of 'Monument' would've worked equally well as a *Quartet* track, perhaps opening side two in preference to 'Visions In Blue'.

'Break Your Back' (Cann, Cross, Currie, Ure) 3:27

Released as the B-side to 'Visions In Blue', 'Break Your Back' was a questionable moment for 1980s Ultravox fans. It wilfully aped US hip hop and rap, an electro-breakdance mix complete with random rhythms, laser blasts and Warren Cann's mutterings. It's the kind of thing the Art of Noise and Trevor Horn (Malcolm McLaren's 'Buffalo Gals') were doing so much better, and for Ultravox, this proved to be a failed experiment: a random, scattershot and stiff attempt at funk, and an arena they never returned to (Rightly so!).

'Overlook' (Cann, Cross, Currie, Ure) 4:04

Rhythmically similar, this B-side to 'We Came To Dance' is a better-crafted take on the 'Break Your Back' idea, with a proper melody and some abstract vocals. It's certainly more musically accomplished, but that's not saying much.

Lament (1984)

Personnel:
Midge Ure: lead vocals, guitar
Warren Cann: drums, electronic percussion, backing vocals
Billy Currie: violin, keyboards
Chris Cross: bass, synthesizers, backing vocals
Mae McKenna: Gaelic vocals ('Man Of Two Worlds')
String quartet: Amanda Woods, Jacky Woods, Margaret Roseberry, Robert Woollard ('Heart Of The Country')
Shirley Roden, Debi Doss: backing vocals ('A Friend I Call Desire')
Producer: Ultravox
Recorded at Musicfest, London
Label: Chrysalis
Release date: 6 April 1984 (UK)
Charts: UK: 8, US: 115, AUS: 41, BEL: 5, CAN: 58, FRA: 43, HOL: 42, GER 27, ICE: 8, IRE: 16, NZ: 7, Nl: 13, NOR: 10, SWE: 8
Running time: 37:29

With George Martin having polished Ultravox into a more pop-oriented outfit, they decided to produce their next album themselves. They'd draw on the lessons learned from Martin and Plank, and Cross, Currie and Cann could invoke their earlier work with Brian Eno and Steve Lillywhite. Midge Ure and Billy Currie had both built their own home studios (Ure's Musicfest in Chiswick and Currie's Hot Food in the basement of his Notting Hill Home).

Despite all their chart success, tensions were beginning to show, perhaps as a result of that success. Ure's hit solo cover of The Walker Brothers' 'No Regrets' (which reached number nine in the UK in June 1982, spending ten weeks in the chart) and his 1983 single 'After A Fashion' with Japan's Mick Karn (39, with four weeks in the chart) had indicated to Currie that Ure was beginning to think about pursuing a solo career – which would have implications for the entire band. Arguably, Ure's contributions helped turn the band from a critically appreciated art-rock outfit into a reliable hit-making machine. Currie was probably right to worry about a future without Ure's involvement, feeling unhappy that the band's success appeared to rest upon the involvement of their charismatic frontman. In a 1985 *Sound On Sound* interview, Ure commented: 'I originally talked about doing a solo album when I released my first solo single, but I never found the time'.

In late-1983 into early-1984, Ultravox reconvened to develop their seventh studio album, ultimately titled *Lament*. It was their fourth album with Ure. Much of the material was co-written by Ure and Cross at the Isle of Lewis, the largest of Scotland's Outer Hebrides islands. Their experience would feed into the distinct Celtic nature of the album's songs and also the sleeve design. Other unique elements were added to the band's expanding sound, including the string quartet on 'Heart Of The Country', and female backing vocals on

'Man Of Two Worlds' (in Gaelic) and 'A Friend I Call Desire'. These elements helped make *Lament* distinct from the previous three LPs. Little did anyone involved know that one track from the album would provide the band with their biggest hit since 'Vienna'.

The band's design and approach to their look – especially on the *Monument* tour – was the focus of an episode of Channel 4's *Design Matters* programme in 1984. It looked at how a rock band employed design elements in creating their brand. Ure, Cann and Currie discussed the casual division of responsibilities that the band employed. Cann explained: 'We've found that the best people to get across what we're about is ourselves ... We'll come up with three or four basic concepts for a stage design, then go to professional stage designers and have them organise our ideas for us'. Peter Saville backed this up by pointing out that while the band all had ideas of their own, they 'were quite receptive to other ideas. They use me to visualise some of the things they're interested in, and I put in things that I'm interested in, and together we get a result.' The programme highlighted how important image and design were to the pop and rock world of the mid-1980s, and Ultravox were fortunate to be chosen as a focus.

A West End theatre stage design inspired Ure and Saville in the creation of the monument motif that ran through the *Quartet* album and its singles, as well as the live album and video *Monument*. Saville explained that the stage set for the *Monument* tour came first, and it was then disassembled into its constituent parts to provide the graphic imagery that ran across all the *Quartet*-related releases throughout 1982/1983 and into the following *Set Movements* tour. Ure told *Event* magazine: 'When Ultravox made *Lament*, we talked about having the entire sleeve black. My argument was that it's minimal advertising, and people would say, 'Wow, what's this?'. Then Spinal Tap did *Smell The Glove* – 'None more black' – and it was rubbish. A close escape'.

Lament became another gold-selling album, though it only reached eight in the UK. The album spent 26 weeks on the chart – 18 in the top 40, five in the top 20 and two in the top ten. It was the band's fourth consecutive top-ten album. US magazine *Trouser Press* gave it a positive write-up: 'Ultravox self-produced *Lament*, proving themselves quite capable of working without outside supervision. The album contains two of their finest singles – 'One Small Day' and 'Dancing With Tears In My Eyes', amidst a host of other suave and personable excursions. *Lament* further elevates Ultravox's reputation as one of the few groups to capably incorporate synthesizers and other modern conveniences into a truly unique sound'.

In a similar vein, the American *Rolling Stone* passed its verdict on *Lament*: 'Of all the bands that still survive from the New Romantics movement of 1980-81, Ultravox is making music that's closest to its original style – a mixture of electronic and conventional instruments ... in which the vocals take a back seat to the beat ... *Lament* may seem a bit less aurally complicated than this quartet's earlier efforts, but its glossy Euro sound is icily appealing all the same. Ultravox may think it's on the cutting edge, but many of this album's moments are Blitz Club circa 1980. At its best, *Lament* sounds like the first nostalgic techno-pop record'.

'White China' (Cann, Cross, Currie, Ure) 3:50

The first indications that *Lament* would be driven by what Dave Thompson (allmusic.com) dubbed 'furious rhythms' came on the unlikely opening track 'White China' (unlikely because the following track, 'One Small Day,' feels like a perfect album opener). The rhythm opens the track with electronic percussion inserts topped by Cann's live drumming. Ure's singing is a little soft and diffuse (and his sampled voice chanting 'We stand to fall' in the background doesn't help), but the lyric tells a clear story that's open to interpretation. There are suggestions of totalitarianism, possibly inspired by the negotiations over the planned 1999 handover of Hong Kong from Britain to China. The rise of China as a world power throughout the 1980s gave this song strong contemporary relevance, and it has lost none of that relevance.

The colour suggestions running throughout ('When pale turns to pink/With a soft unnerving ease', 'When white turns to red/In the not-too-distant days') are open to reds-under-the-bed interpretations. The future subjugation of other parts of the world under Chinese Communism is suggested in 'Will force and misery be the life you have to lead?' and 'When the freedom slips away'. That last ominous line indicates that such loss of freedom is not an overnight event but a slow process, perhaps over decades (giving 'White China' relevance now). That straightforward reading can be augmented by a couple of other angles. The teen-angst angle is never far from Ultravox's songs (after all, that's who was buying the records in the 1980s), and that offers a secondary interpretation for lines like 'With your future in another's hands/When your life is not your own', equating parental control to nationalist totalitarianism. Finally, given the fact that in the early 1980s, the most common type of heroin found in Britain was dubbed 'China white', perhaps 'White China' can be seen as a drug song, with the loss of freedom alluding to addiction. Either way, it's a sparkling track that's driven by its unique rhythmic experimentation, prioritising sequencer and drum machine effects.

Unlike most of the *Lament* tracks, 'White China' is heavy on digital synths, with guitar work entirely absent. For the first (but not last) time, there is something of a New Order sound here (as on the album closer 'A Friend I Call Desire'), suggesting their 'Bizarre Love Triangle' released two years later owed something (especially rhythmically) to Ultravox. The 'Special Mix' version extended the track, coming in at over eight minutes long, with much clearer, stronger, untreated and separated vocals. Ure recalled: 'We wanted to release 'White China'. European territories wanted us to put out 'Dancing...''. We all thought it was an album track; it was too obvious to us in a way and it was instantly dismissed as a single. [It] would have meant two videos, two budgets, and with the tour coming up, we didn't have the time'. 'White China' was dropped as a single idea in favour of 'Dancing With Tears In My Eyes', which unexpectedly reached number three in the UK!

'One Small Day' (Cann, Cross, Currie, Ure) 4:30
Guitars are very much to the fore from the beginning. This rocking track perhaps should've been the album opener, especially as it was the first single. Out on 26 January 1984, it reached 27 in the UK in late February (spending six weeks in the chart), breaking Ultravox's uninterrupted run of eight top 20 hit singles in a row (excluding the reissued 'Slow Motion') from 'Vienna' to 'We Came To Dance'. Perhaps the guitar-heavy rock sound was too different from most of what had come before. It's a powerhouse track that put the band on par with the likes of U2 and Big Country, but perhaps it took a while to be appreciated.

From the surprising opening guitar lick and the thumping drums, 'One Small Day' doesn't sound at all like traditional Ultravox until Ure's vocal comes in. It's an obvious – if catchy – passionate song about achieving your potential and fighting against obstacles. The upbeat rhythm matches the sentiments in the chorus:

One day where I didn't die a thousand times
Where I could satisfy this life of mine
One day where every hour could be a joy to me
And live a life the way it's meant to be

The obstacles to this wonderful life are just as obvious – lack of time ('If the stack is high against you/And the hammer's coming down'); low mood ('How many times have you let depression win the fight?') and lack of support ('How many times will they walk away?').

Ultravox appear to have adopted a 1980s stadium-rock guise here – all the more obvious when it's remembered that this was one of four songs they played at Live Aid on 13 July 1985 (in front of a 72,000-strong audience at Wembley). Those songs were selected for being more easily performed live without much requirement for synthesizers, so their two biggest hit singles ('Vienna' and 'Dancing With Tears In My Eyes') were supported by the rock sound of 'One Small Day' and the unlikely opener 'Reap The Wild Wind'. Despite the terror that Ure described feeling in his autobiography *If I Was*, it's clear from the footage of their 18-minute set that they were in their element (especially a particularly bouncy Currie and a beaming Cross). It's hard to imagine the John Foxx Ultravox playing on that day.

The 'One Small Day' video was shot in extremely cold conditions over a January weekend at the Callanish standing stones on the Isle of Skye, where Ure and Cross had drawn much of their inspiration for the *Lament* material. The video opens with shots of the stones against an atmospheric wind sound before the guitar and drums crash in. The performance was augmented by *2001: A Space Odyssey*-style landscape shots (reflected in a mirror), the band themselves caught in huge vertical, triangular mirrors. Each member was clad for the cold weather conditions! Blended in over the landscape shots were sped-up clips from many of the band's previous videos.

Smash Hits dubbed the track 'a typically melodramatic Ultravox single, with a soaring chorus and a matinee-idol performance from Midge Ure ... This time there's some heavy electric-guitar-playing to the fore' (recalling Ure's stint with Thin Lizzy). *Record Mirror* boasted that the week's singles would be 'rubbished' by Morrissey. He didn't disappoint with his take on 'One Small Day': 'This might not be the worst record in the universe, but it's certainly in the running'.

'Dancing With Tears In My Eyes' (Cann, Cross, Currie, Ure) 4:39

The threat of nuclear annihilation hung over the 1980s as the Cold War continued at full strength. That prospect became the subject of multiple pop and rock tracks of the era, including Frankie Goes to Hollywood ('Two Tribes'), Nena ('99 Red Balloons') and Iron Maiden ('Two Minutes To Midnight'). Ultravox joined the atomic-annihilation jukebox (by association) with the anthemic 'Dancing With Tears In My Eyes', released as a single in May 1984. The timing was perfect, giving the band their second greatest hit after 'Vienna'. The new single spent 13 weeks in the UK chart (eight in the top 40), peaking at number three on 9 June 1984.

The lyric was actually about a nuclear power plant meltdown (and thematically about loss) but was widely interpreted as being about the end of the world due to an exchange of nuclear missiles between the great superpowers. Ure had been inspired by the 1957 Neville Shute novel *On The Beach*, which was made into a movie in 1959. The novel sees a group of people stranded in Australia, awaiting nuclear annihilation thanks to an atomic war in the Northern Hemisphere. Ure told *Glide* magazine in 2018: 'They knew it was the end, but they had time to think about how they wanted to choose their final moments, and that's what 'Dancing With Tears In My Eyes' was about'.

The number three chart placing was a dramatic recovery from the poor performance of 'One Small Day' (number 27) after the strong run of top 20 singles from *Rage In Eden* and *Quartet*. It had been three years since 'Vienna' almost topped the charts, and the new single proved that Ultravox still had what it took. It was a success across Europe, hitting the top ten in Belgium (two), Germany (seven), Holland (six) and Poland (six). It failed to crack the US *Billboard* Hot 100, stalling at 108. The hoped-for big breakthrough in the US never really came.

The single's success was helped hugely by an iconic video directed by Ure and Cross, which got significant television airtime. The video depicted clearly that the danger came from the meltdown of a nuclear power plant and not an exchange of nuclear missiles as popularly supposed. It depicts Cross, Cann and Currie as workers and a police officer at the power plant, seemingly unable to prevent the catastrophic meltdown. Ure is depicted as a man driving home to be with his wife (played by Diana Weston, later known for her role in British 1990s sitcom *The Upper Hand*) while hearing the news of the impending disaster on the radio ('the wireless'). The climax comes as the power plant explodes, the impact of which is seen from within the domestic home. It was this contrast of the domestic setting and everyday activities with the end of the world in a nuclear fire that made the video (and the song) so powerful and, therefore, so popular. The video fades on celluloid home movies (perhaps the 'tapes you might leave behind' from 'All Stood Still': Ultravox's other nuclear-hell top ten hit) burning in the inferno. This scenario was inspired by the 1979 Three Mile Island nuclear power plant meltdown in the US and pre-dated the 1986 Chernobyl nuclear explosion by a couple of years. The video complimented the BBC's screening of the horrifying nuclear aftermath drama *Threads* in September 1984, just months after the video came out.

The song was later included in the soundtrack for the 2015 video game *Metal Gear Solid V – The Phantom Pain*. The track also appeared in the 2015 sports documentary *Prois Tartan* (which chronicled the world's oldest football fixture, a match between Scotland and England) and in the 2015 Italian movie *Ride*, about a family coping with the death of their father. The track also featured in the final episode of the 2019 comedy-drama *White Gold*, about a window salesman in 1983.

Almost as guitar heavy as 'One Small Day', 'Dancing With Tears In My Eyes' was much more instantly recognisable as an Ultravox song, riding the contemporary news headlines about the belligerence of US President Ronald Regan, the arrival on UK soil of American Cruise missiles, and the ratcheting up of Cold War tension. Alongside the prominent guitar was a pulsing synth-bass part. Like many of the tracks on *Lament*, the song lacked a signature Currie solo moment.

The single sleeve was a still image from the video (the window and curtains blown in by the blast) fragmented by the box grid pattern also seen on the *Lament* album sleeve. Highly visible in the video's domestic living room is an American flag.

The song did beat Frankie Goes to Hollywood's similarly themed 'Two Tribes' into the charts by a whole two months. Where Frankie took a comic-book approach with their video depicting Reagan and Gorbachev in a wrestling ring, Ultravox went for a kind of designer nuclear anxiety: a much more tasteful approach to the end of the world.

'Lament' (Cann, Cross, Currie, Ure) 4:40
The title track (released on 21 June 1984 as the album's third and final single) was another attempt at a slow ballad in the style of 'Vienna' and 'Visions In

Blue'. It failed to ride the crest of the wave of the previous ode to nuclear annihilation, reaching only number 22 in the UK, but spending eight weeks in the chart, five of them in the top 40.

It had a very different but equally strong music video, shot on the Isle of Skye and featuring a romantic storyline in which each of the visiting band members is paired off with a local lassie to enjoy a holiday romance. Ure commented in the *Design Matters* documentary: 'If you've got the facilities and you've got the ability to control all aspects of what you're doing, then I think you should exercise that right. We've been lucky enough to gain that confidence from our record company, so we can go off and direct our own videos because they know we can do it now'. Ure commented specifically on the 'Lament' video:

> It's a feel we're after rather than a storyline. The last video had a very strong storyline, and that was the strength of it. Everyone was expecting a 'Dancing With Tears' mark two, and they're not going to get that with this. This song was written up here, and the feel of the music is very Scottish, with lilting, haunting melodies. What we want is visuals to go with that, featuring the dramatic countryside that we have here, and we've already tied that in with the graphics on the single sleeve. The idea is that four guys meet four girls in this wondrous holiday hideaway.

The video – shot in the villages of Elgol and Kilmarie – climaxes with a joyful Ceilidh (in Hallapool's Broadford Hall) – quite a contrast to the positively frightening 'Dancing With Tears In My Eyes', even if the romance of 'Lament' is only fleeting and can't last (though Midge does get to stay behind with his girl when the others leave!).

The song's mournful and elegiac nature (fitting for an album track) possibly worked against its potential success as a single. It simply lacked the rousing nature of its two predecessors (though it charted slightly higher than 'One Small Day'). A fitting antidote to the nuclear horrors of 'Dancing With Tears In My Eyes'.

'Man Of Two Worlds' (Cann, Cross, Currie, Ure) 4:27

The Scottish vibe continues into the strong opener of side two. After a guitar-heavy first side, the synths are to the fore once more, though the sedate opening suggests another slow-moving piece as the rhythms and Currie's delicate piano soon come in.

Mae McKenna provided the Gaelic singing, giving a Clannad-like sound. (Female backing vocals were to return on 'A Friend I Call Desire' and across the following album *U-Vox*). The Gaelic translates as 'Hand in hand, taste the past/As I drink in this gift to me/Hand in hand, taste the past/As I drink from it all'. The lyric connects to Scottish myth, carried over from 'Lament', with Ure singing 'Taking shelter by the standing stones/Miles from all that moves' and 'Feeling spirits never far removed/Passing over me and I greet them with open arms'. 'Standing stones' ties in with the images on the *Lament* packaging and to the music video for 'One Small Day'. In effect, 'Man of Two Worlds' anticipates the *Outlander* book and 2014 television series, which saw a woman from 1945 transported back to 1743 while visiting some standing stones. Ure's closing verse – 'Feel a presence moving into me/Painting pictures with its words/Seeing places that I've never seen/Like a door thrown open on a life I've lived before' – suggests such mystical intervention, as if a doorway has been opened onto the past, or even hints of reincarnation. It's the Gaelic singing reinforcing those mystical themes that really makes the song stand out, as Currie's synth work is subdued, and the guitar, when it does appear, is a little underpowered. Otherwise, Ultravox were beginning to verge on folk-pop here.

'Heart Of The Country' (Cann, Cross, Currie, Ure) 5:05
Released as a single in September 1984 in Germany only, 'Heart Of The Country' appears to play with ideas of patriotism and devotion to country: something believed in but eventually soured. It's expanded with a string quartet, adding significant depth, presumably under the direction of the classically trained Currie.

Built around the rhythms – as much of *Lament* was, with Cann's experimental percussion breaks much more to the fore than ever – the song almost dispenses with traditional structure altogether. Many Ultravox songs begin with the chorus, breaking with the standard verse-chorus-verse structure, but 'Heart Of The Country' doesn't appear to have a chorus, relying instead on the rhythm to maintain a structure and forward momentum. Dave Thompson (allmusic.com) said of this track: "Heart Of The Country' is built not on a melody but a riff. Nor is there any sign of a hook and only the barest outline of a chorus. However, the song's glory is in its entrancing atmosphere and the mesmerising rhythm that hypnotically casts its spell over the listener'. Ure's vocal also helps to ground the track, playing up the shift from uncritical belief ('I was young and not deceived then/I believed in the heart of the country') to disillusionment ('Then I saw through the charade/The facade, now I've had it all', 'I am older, I am wiser/I despise the heart of the country').

The instrumental version on the 'Lament' B-side (there was also an 11-minute 'Special Re-Mix' available) lets the track breathe, allowing proper appreciation of the classic Ultravox instrumentation, something previously central to their sound but missing from much of side one. 'Heart Of The Country' cautiously edges towards some of the atmospheric work that dominated *Rage In Eden*.

'When The Time Comes' (Cann, Cross, Currie, Ure) 4:56
Straightforward relationship songs were largely absent from *Lament* (and much of the Ultravox canon). The armageddon angst of 'Dancing With Tears

In My Eyes' and the music video holiday romance of 'Lament' were about all that was on offer until this song turned up. In fact, it's about the ending of a relationship, with propulsive verses and a tense, sharp vocal.

After the gentle opening, the music turns harsher (echoing the emotional content), playing out over Cross's Japan-style fretless bass-playing. Cann's airy percussion backs everything up, but this is very much driven by the bass and Currie's synths (echoing some of 'Visions In Blue' and anticipating the brass on *U-Vox*). The instrumental break gives Currie a brief chance to shine, but it's still that all-consuming bass that stands out. The soaring vocal, as the track begins to fade away, puts a positive gloss on this tale of relationships doomed.

'A Friend I Call Desire' (Cann, Cross, Currie, Ure) 5:09
Reminiscent of Joy Division and post-Ian Curtis follow-up band New Order, 'A Friend I Called Desire' boasted some interesting guitar work and rhythms but was a weak closer for *Lament* (echoing the quartet *Quartet* closer 'The Song (We Go)', but without the innovative percussion finale later appended to 'The Voice' when played live).

The 'work in progress' mix (actually an instrumental), released on a later reissue, reveals the strength of the track's musical basis. What made the finished version stand out was the up-front female vocals: seemingly a most un-Ultravox sound at the time. The band's traditional instrumentation seems better here, with an uplifting lilt to the whole thing.

The lyric plays effectively with various permutations of the concept of desire (love, sex, material things, success) and the way it can become a self-damaging obsession: 'The torch I carried, burnt my hand'. The rhythmic and climactic vocal ('And the pain and the lust/And the want and the hurt/And the lies and the fear/And the urge and the feel/And the touch') takes things out on a solid note. The individual elements all seem to be there, but when put together, the final *Lament* song fails to live up to its promise.

Related Tracks
'Easterly' (Cann, Cross, Currie, Ure) 3:49
Released as the B-side of 'One Small Day', 'Easterly' is an instrumental that sounds like it was an excuse to play around with the new digital technology (which had seemingly weakened Currie's overall synth sounds compared to the analogue synths on *Vienna* and *Rage In Eden*). Throughout *Lament*, exotic rhythms are to the fore, drawing on Eastern sounds. By 1984, the instrumentals that once formed a core part of the band's output ('Astradyne' and much of the extended instrumentation on *Rage In Eden*) had become like Midge Ure solo throwaway tracks. Even their titles – 'Mood Music' and 'Textures' – reveal the approach. There is, however, an echo here of the work of Be-Bop Deluxe's Bill Nelson – especially 'Secret Ceremony', which was used as the theme to the 1987 series *Brond*.

'Building' (Cann, Cross, Currie, Ure) 3:14

The B-side to the hit single 'Dancing With Tears In My Eyes', 'Building' is another track that has just enough echoes of some of the elements – and certainly the mood – that made up *Rage In Eden* to make it worthwhile. It's built around Currie's emotional piano playing, augmented by Ure's straining vocal, attempting a Frank Sinatra impersonation. It actually sounds more like a David Sylvian track than anything by Ultravox or Ure solo – slow and contemplative, depending on the lyric to provide the emotional heft in counterpoint to the piano.

Possibly – depending on the lyric interpretation – this would be the third track in a row (following 'When The Time Comes' and 'A Friend I Call Desire') dealing with a disintegrating relationship. It's an effective B-side experiment, showcasing a different side of the Ultravox sound that was never followed up on in any depth, making 'Building' a unique cut.

'Rivets' (Cann, Cross, Currie, Ure) 0:57

Levi's sponsored the *Set Movements* tour that saw Ultravox take up a five-night residency at the Hammersmith Odeon in June 1984. This allowed the band to include an audio commentary on cassette along with their usual deluxe-printed programme. This featured the slightly longer cinema version of 'Rivets' – a Cross/Ure creation for use in a 1983 Levi's TV commercial – along with instrumental versions of various *Lament* tracks. Not included on the cassette was the shorter version of 'Rivets' used in the award-winning TV commercial. Both cuts of the ad (which can be found on YouTube) depicted the creation of the distinctive Levi jeans rivets, from the unearthing of the raw materials through the refinement of the ore to their stamping into the finished jeans. Subsequently commissioned to provide music for the follow-up ad 'Threads', Ure and Cross withdrew their involvement after one too many requests for revisions. Composed by someone else attempting to ape their sound, the follow-up commercial bombed and 'Rivets' returned to TV shortly afterwards. Their efforts on the withdrawn submission weren't wasted – the basic riff for 'Threads' was later expanded and built on to create the non-album Ultravox single 'Love's Great Adventure'.

'Love's Great Adventure' (Cann, Cross, Currie, Ure) 3:04

Yet another different side to Ultravox was revealed in the 'Love's Great Adventure' stand-alone single, released on 12 October 1984 to promote the career-spanning *The Collection* compilation released on 2 November 1984. The single reached 12 in the UK, staying there for two weeks in November, sticking around for nine weeks and spending seven in the top 40. It was to be the group's last top-20 hit. *The Collection* spent 53 weeks in the UK chart, peaking at number two twice, spending 13 weeks in the top ten, 16 in the top 20 and 21 in the top 40. It proved to be the band's highest-charting album, reaching triple-platinum status in excess of 900,000 copies. It was the 11th best-selling album of 1984.

The single – their 13th top 30 single in a row – was a deliberate attempt to show a different side to their temperament, and it enjoyed huge radio airplay. Currie explained the genesis and creation of the track to *Electronics & Music Maker* magazine in October 1984:

> We wanted to do something different, to get out of the way singles are taken from an album ... when any band puts out several singles from the same album, they might appear to be very different in some ways, but because they were all recorded at the same time, they have the same feel to them. We wanted to get away from that and do a one-off single that was totally separate from any album. The recording was a lot more immediate than *Lament*. We decided not to go into the studio and spend a long time doing it because things can become really sluggish when you're doing albums. For the single, there was plenty of momentum ... and the momentum thing is important. Having done the single like that, I'd now like to do an album in the same way – do it with just a couple of days of rehearsals or none at all, which was what we did for the single.

Warren Cann also explained how he contrived to make the track upbeat: 'It's in threes, and it's got a very up, happy melody, which is why we decided to persevere with it in the first place. We'd tried things in that time signature before, but they'd always sounded contrived, but this one doesn't. There's no real technical trickery in making it; it's the strength of the song that carries it through.'

The single was boosted hugely by a highly amusing video from Cross and Ure. While the 'Reap The Wild Wind' video had featured Warren Cann pausing briefly in front of a *Raiders Of The Lost Ark* poster, the 'Love's Great Adventure' video riffed wholesale on the Indiana Jones adventure movies. Shot in Kenya, it featured Ure as a pony-tailed comic-book reader who falls into a fantasy *Boy's Own*-type adventure where he is in pursuit of a millionaire lost in the jungle. Along the way, he runs into various problems (snakes, armed mercenaries, native warriors), only to be rescued by fellow adventurers Cann and Cross and Currie as a missionary priest who rescues all three when they're staked out in the desert. The millionairess is finally found and rescued (after a paragliding sequence, complete with an Indiana Jones-style animated map), only for Ure's girlfriend to bring him back to the present from his dream, when he's given a chance to be a real hero, fighting off a gang of thieving bullies. Annabel Giles – Ure's girlfriend and later wife (they married in 1985, divorced in 1989; Giles died of brain cancer in 2023, aged 64) – reappeared as the millionairess, perhaps positioning this as a sequel to 'Lament' (which she also featured in). The photo she has of the two of them together looks suspiciously like it could be from that earlier video. An additional humorous touch is the pause when Ure finds himself out of breath; the music stops as he recovers, then resumes, yet this comes a mere 30 seconds into the exhausting adventure!

The song and the video certainly stuck in the mind of the creators of *Inside No. 9* – the macabre anthology show by Steve Pemberton and Reece Shearsmith. In 2010, they titled series five episode three 'Love's Great Adventure' – a semi-improvised instalment, and they used the song over the closing credits.

As a one-off, upbeat celebration of Ultravox in promotion of their greatest hits collection, 'Love's Great Adventure' did the trick. It would mark a high point – musically and in chart terms – that the band would not reach again.

U-Vox (1986)

Personnel:
Midge Ure: lead vocals, guitar
Billy Currie: violin, keyboards, synthesizers
Chris Cross: bass, synthesizers, backing vocals
Mark Brzezicki: drums
Carol Kenyon: backing vocals ('Same Old Story', 'The Prize')
Kevin Powell: bass ('Sweet Surrender')
Beggar & Co: brass ('Same Old Story')
Derek Watkins, Gary Barnacle, John Thirkell, Pete Thoms: brass ('The Prize')
The Chieftains: backing musicians ('All Fall Down')
George Martin: arranger, conductor ('All Fall Down')
Producers: Conny Plank, Ultravox
Recorded at Conny Plank's Studio, Cologne, West Germany; Hot Food, Music
Fest, West Side, and AIR (London), Windmill Lane (Dublin)
Label: Chrysalis
Release date: 9 October 1986 (UK)
Charts: UK: 9, AUS: 92, FRA: 44, GER: 49, NL: 49, SWE: 16, SWI: 29
Running time: 42:49

The Ultravox that recorded the controversial 1986 album *U-Vox* was a
changed band. It was the fifth and final album (to that point) to feature
their 1979 lineup, although one member was lost along the way. Featuring
a notable change in sound, the album failed to appeal to the band's core
fans, with many disparaging it as 'the pink thing' thanks to its distinctive,
divisive packaging. Despite that, *U-Vox* sold well, reaching number nine in
the UK, their seventh album in a row to crack the top ten, including the 1983
live compilation *Monument* (nine) and 1984's *The Collection*, which reached
number two and spent over a year in the charts. Even the 1993 compilation
If I Was: The Very Best Of Midge Ure & Ultravox reached number ten. It was a
solid track record, but Ultravox would not trouble the higher reaches of the
album chart again until 2012's reunion project *Brilliant* (which peaked at 21).

Following 1984's *Lament*, the band were on a renewed high, having
reached number three in the UK with 'Dancing With Tears In My Eyes'.
However, there were growing tensions – particularly between Ure and Currie
– over their musical direction. With two top 40 solo hits ('No Regrets' and
'After A Fashion'), Ure's thoughts were moving beyond Ultravox, though
it seems he also realised that the band gave him a solid base to further his
musical exploration.

Currie had become increasingly concerned about Ure's control, with
Lament, in particular, beginning to move in a more Celtic direction, away
from the more esoteric focus of *Vienna* and *Rage In Eden*. While the George
Martin-produced *Quartet* had given the band a slicker, smoother sound
(and a series of top 20 hits), Currie wasn't entirely happy with the direction

86

things were moving in. Equally frustrated was drummer Warren Cann, who'd expressed a desire to move beyond simply providing the band's rhythmic underpinning (which he felt he'd pushed as far as he could with his experimentation on *Lament*). Cann wanted to take up guitar and become more involved in the band's musical development. As Ure was lead guitarist, with Cross on bass, an additional guitarist perhaps seemed surplus to requirements. These issues all came to a head when the band reconvened to record *U-Vox*.

In the meantime, Ure – alongside The Boomtown Rats' Bob Geldof – had become one of the faces of the Band Aid charity project that aimed to help alleviate famine in Ethiopia. Ure and Geldof co-wrote the charity record 'Do They Know It's Christmas?' and produced the single, which gathered many contemporary mid-1980s pop talents together. The single entered the UK chart at number one in December 1984, selling in excess of 1,000,000 in the first week, remaining there for five weeks. Record sales worldwide raised £8,000,000 for the charity. Ure and Geldof then established the Band Aid Trust and set up the July 1985 international Live Aid event. Thanks to Ure's participation, Ultravox featured prominently at Live Aid.

Taking advantage of his charity-related success and fame, Ure finally took the plunge on a solo career, releasing the single 'If I Was' (co-written by Ure and The Messengers' Danny Mitchell) in September 1985, which reached number one in the UK in October, followed by two weeks at number two (the single spending 14 weeks on the chart, ten in the top 40). His debut solo album *The Gift* followed in October 1985, peaking at two in its first week, spending 15 weeks in the chart overall.

There can be no denying that Band Aid, Live Aid and Ure's 1985 solo success changed him. He returned to Ultravox with a different outlook toward the band and the wider world. In the Ultravox fanzine *Extreme Voice* #10 (1991), Ure admitted: 'The spark kind of went out of it for me. Live Aid and Band Aid had a lot to do with it, I suppose. We had a long break from each other, and when we came back together, we were all working in different directions. It just kind of died like anything, like a relationship. We took such a long break'. In his autobiography *If I Was*, Ure noted that in his absence, the rest of the band had been working in Currie's studio, producing new music that Ure found 'very dated and random'. He said that in the two years since *Lament*, the 'musical climate' had changed: 'Where Ultravox had once been cutting edge, synthesizers and electronic drums were now everywhere. The solo stuff I'd been doing was simple, but everything in Ultravox seemed so complicated'. The band's interpersonal problems ultimately led to drummer Warren Cann exiting the collective before the recording of *U-Vox*. Ure admitted:

On *Vienna*, Warren had written a good chunk of the lyrics, but on subsequent albums, I didn't want him to. I wanted to sing my own lyrics, so he must've felt pushed out, even though we split four ways … There are always tensions within a group. One of the facts of life is that the lead singer will always garner more attention than the drummer … nobody wants to interview the drummer. Billy, too, sometimes resented my role as frontman. By 1986, Ultravox was heading off on four separate paths.

Recognising that things had to change, the four members held a meeting to clear the air. Ure wanted to return to the *Vienna* setup, dropping Cann's complicated drum machines. They agreed to try it, but according to Ure, when they assembled for rehearsal, Cann arrived with all his drum machines. Ure claimed, 'He wouldn't pick up his sticks. He was more interested in drum machines than in hitting his skins. He'd rather spend hours programming, laboriously hitting buttons … We needed the looseness, the flexibility of a human drummer'. Though Ure, Cross and Currie agreed that Cann had to go, it was down to Ure to do what he called 'the dirty work':

I couldn't look at him, only down at the carpet as I said, 'Sorry, Warren, you're not in the band anymore'. Warren was shell-shocked, as he hadn't seen it coming at all. When he got the news … he just got up and walked out. It was a very dignified exit … He was one of the founding members and had been playing with Chris and Billy for 12 years and me for seven … The band was already finished, but we didn't realise it. We needed a scapegoat, so we took it out on Warren … We thought it was a whole new start … (but) the foundations were gone. Sacking Warren was the beginning of the end.

Cann revealed his take on the situation in a 1986 interview for the *In The City* fanzine (conducted by Peter Gilbert and Frank Drake and republished in *Extreme Voice* #13): 'In a few short words, I was sacked. It was a complete surprise to me'. Cann blamed the changes in the band's outlook on their lack of success in America and the long break they took between albums. While Ure and Currie kept busy with their own projects (Ure also got married), Cross and Cann were left hanging in the wind. 'I was getting bored … Midge was doing his solo tour … We were all adamant that the album should have a completely different sound, a drastic change … That perked me up and I threw myself into it wholeheartedly … When Midge came back, everything changed … The stuff I liked the most was the stuff he liked the least … I was really shocked, stunned and dazed … It was just laid on me'. The other three saw Cann as being out of step with their musical direction. There was no other option laid on the table but Cann's departure. Most of all, Cann was hurt by the radio silence that followed: 'Nobody's subsequently been in touch with me … With Midge, the relationship was just a work one, but with Chris and Bill, it was different because we'd been together a lot longer … None of them, privately, said to me, "I'm sorry. I wish it could have worked out another way"'.

In an attempt to recapture past glories, the remaining three decided to re-engage Conny Plank as producer – a move 'back to when it was fresh and exciting' claimed Ure. *U-Vox* was recorded in the studios of Currie and Ure in London and Plank in Germany, with the album mixed at Montserrat (as was the case on *Quartet*). Shortly after the first mixing sessions, Plank fell ill while touring South America. It was the first sign of the laryngeal cancer that ultimately killed him in December 1987, aged just 47. Deciding the initial *U-Vox* mixes were 'dead and flat', the band recruited John Hudson and Rik Walton to further work on the mixes.

Despite being a hit record, Ure came to regard *U-Vox* as a mistake. He noted in his autobiography: 'The last Ultravox album was called *U-Vox*. We should have called it *U-bend* because it should have gone down the drain. It deserved to. It was an album that should never have been'. The band were too focused on pursuing their own individual interests, so the album never came together as a coherent work. Each track represented different factions and various ideas of the future sound of Ultravox, with individual members pulling in different, often contradictory, directions. Currie's interest in orchestral work resulted in 'All In One Day', while Ure's messianic save-the-world complex came out on 'All Fall Down'. He told *Extreme Voice* in 1991: 'We were all working in different directions. You could see the splits. I was thinking of working with The Chieftains, and I did, and it was so un-Ultravoxy. A lot of bands stick together for the wrong reasons ... We all decided to let it die a graceful death'.

The band were committed to a tour, but Ure decided he'd had enough. He agreed to complete the tour, but after that, he'd be exiting Ultravox: 'There was an Ultravox before me. There's no reason why there can't be an Ultravox after me'. Chris Cross felt the same, but according to Ure, Billy Currie took the dissolution of the band – for the second time – rather badly. Ure agreed to Currie retaining the Ultravox name if he wanted, as 'I had no rights to it at all'. Looking back, Ure admitted he hadn't been prepared for the personal fallout that his leaving Ultravox would cause. However, he did look back on all that Ultravox had achieved since 1979 with a sense of pride: 'We were lucky enough to forge something very special together and make fantastic sounds. It became successful, which gave everyone a great income. It was weird towards the end but brilliant at the beginning. It was the best thing I ever did, to spend seven years in a great band with a bunch of mates and travel all around the world'.

Almost two decades on from the *U-Vox* debacle, Ure and the others would remember the *brilliant* beginnings of that successful version of Ultravox when naming their new album.

'Same Old Story' (Cross, Currie, Ure) 4:38
Released on 26 September 1986, this single reached a disappointing 31. Just weeks before the release of the *U-Vox* album, this was the first chance fans

had to hear the band's new direction in the wake of the non-album single 'Love's Great Adventure'.

Cann was missing in action. Instead, heavy brass sounds were to the fore (provided by British funk group Beggar and Co.), along with strong female backing vocals from Carol Kenyon (following similar experiments on *Lament*). Beggar and Co. had their first chart hit in 1981 and regularly provided brass for other artists, including on Spandau Ballet's 'Chant No. 1 (I Don't Need This Pressure On)'. Kenyon had made an impact with her backing vocals on Heaven 17's number two hit 'Temptation' in 1983. She also featured on a variety of records from the likes of Jon and Vangelis, Chris Rea, Dexy's Midnight Runners, Paul Hardcastle and Nik Kershaw. Kenyon also sang on 'The Prize'.

Cann's replacement on drums was Mark Brzezicki – best known for his work as part of Scottish rock outfit Big Country. Brzezicki had played on records by The Cult, Nik Kershaw, Roger Daltrey, Procol Harum and Howard Jones. For Ultravox, Brzezicki was a studio-only musician. On tour and in the 'Same Old Story' video, he was replaced by Pat Ahern (who later directly replaced Brzezicki when he quit Big Country in 1989).

The difference in the Ultravox sound was immediate, with guitar and drums providing a rock edge, with the intrusion of brass marking a key difference, met with Kenyon's opening vocal line. By the time Ure began singing, many fans were wondering exactly what they were listening to. It has an energy, and the brass actually makes for an innovation in the sound., but Brzezicki's drumming is perfunctory, while synth-innovator Currie also appears missing-in-action (something that runs through this album: just where are his keyboard showcases?).

The lines, 'And the sound I hear/Is not the sound I want to hear from you', summed up many initial reactions to this dramatic departure. Perhaps after the 1984 greatest hits album it would be only natural for a band to branch out. For much of the 1980s, brass was very much *in*, so the band might've been following trends rather than creating them as they'd done on *Vienna* and *Rage In Eden*. The thing is, 'Same Old Story' isn't necessarily bad; it's just different. Was it too different to be considered as Ultravox at all?

'Sweet Surrender' (Cross, Currie, Ure) 4:34

Perhaps more reassuring to the diehards was 'Sweet Surrender', which at least boasts a piano/keyboard-driven middle section, even if it's not a patch on Currie's virtuoso synth or violin/viola solos that graced past albums.

The drums-and-brass approach was still very much front-and-centre here, and Brzezicki at least stepped up his percussion work. The vocals and lead guitar work are familiar from more recent Ultravox work (particularly *Quartet*), but the lyric is much more like a Ure solo track. It seems to be about finding the key to unlocking your heart to emotions like love: 'A feeling no one told me could be wild. So wild'. It's simple stuff, boosted by the instrumentation – particularly Kevin Powell's distinctive bass work, which gives it unusual depth. A former member of Steve Harley & Cockney Rebel, Powell had played with Chris Rea and backed Ure on his solo efforts in 1985. This guest-musician policy that runs through *U-Vox* supports the idea in the minds of some critics that far from being an Ultravox album, *U-Vox* was, in fact, another Ure (near) solo effort in which Cross and Currie were simply session musicians alongside the others.

Ure's vocals are the sole linking factor across the album's tracks, but at least on 'Sweet Surrender', he was willing to stretch himself, while the back-to-basics feel of the rest was undoubtedly appealing. Perhaps this track would've been a better single choice than the ponderous 'All Fall Down' and the pretentious 'All In One Day'.

'Dream On' (Cross, Currie, Ure) 4:47

From the fade-in, 'Dream On' anticipates the higher vocal register Ure was to use on the band's 2012 comeback album *Brilliant*. The lyric looks forward to album closer 'All In One Day', anticipating a time 'when there was no fight to fight'. Ure's post-Live Aid lyric obsessions often focused on an amorphous idea of 'world peace' (in counterpoint with the military percussion throughout) – nice to dream about, but hardly likely to happen (as it never has in the history of humanity). The song envisions a world that could 'laugh together', that 'smiles', that 'share(s)' – all very worthy sentiments, but it does make for a rather insipid song.

Musically, it's fine: better than the vocals on top. Cross contributes a hypnotically effective bass part, while Brzezicki's drumming hums along inoffensively (much like the lyric). Another attempt perhaps at the slow-burn style of song that had worked so well in the past (like 'Vienna', 'Visions In Blue' and 'Lament'), 'Dream On' has none of the power of those. At almost five minutes in length, it's the album's longest track to this point, which might account for its hypnotic, droning effect. In the past, a track like this would've been relegated to a B-side and largely forgotten. Instead, it's presented as a showcase, in a position it was simply not worthy of.

'The Prize' (Cross, Currie, Ure) 5:37

The dominant brass of 'Same Old Story' returns, this time played by the quartet of Derek Watkins, Gary Barnacle, John Thirkell and Pete Thoms, with Carol Kenyon again on backing vocals. The strong opening guitar lick is deceptive, as the brass thunders in quickly, with Kenyon's vocal to the fore, dominating Ure.

The prize in question appears to be 'the right to be someone in others' eyes', whatever that might mean. There are obstacles to be overcome – 'dirt and tears', 'the battle of wills', 'the pressures of life' and 'taunts and jokes'. Adam Ant perhaps conveyed the same sentiment better in the 'Prince Charming' line, 'Ridicule is nothing to be ashamed of', but the Ultravox take on the topic suggests that this prize must be worked for in order to be earned. Kenyon is allowed to take over the vocal glories towards the end. Breaching the five-minute mark, 'The Prize' is overly long and outstays what little welcome it had with that opening guitar lick.

More than any other track on *U-Vox*, 'The Prize' commits the popular late-1980s sin of randomly employing brass in order to sound relevant. It might've worked for Duran Duran or Simple Minds, but it doesn't fit Ultravox, no matter how vaguely enjoyable this track might be in isolation. The brass quartet – Watkins and Thirkell (trumpets), Barnacle (saxophone) and Thoms (trombone) – were all session players. Barnacle had appeared on early albums by The Clash (where he was later joined by Pete Thoms), The Ruts, and M's debut album *New York-London-Paris-Munich*. He later played with Simple Minds and Rick Wakeman before forming a horn section for Level 42, bringing in Thirkell. Together, they became known as The Phantom Horns. Barnacle worked with his brother Steve on Visage's second album *The Anvil* in 1982 (which may be where the connection with Ure/Currie originated). Thirkell was a prolific session musician in his own right, performing on hundreds of records for many artists, including with The The's Matt Johnson.

'All Fall Down' (Cross, Currie, Ure) 5:09
With Celtic folk band The Chieftains to the fore, 'All Fall Down' again plays out much more like a solo Ure track. The lyric echos 'Dancing With Tears In My Eyes' in terms of subject matter (nuclear annihilation), and the intention is well meant, but the track is plodding and ponderous, caught up in its own importance while wrapping itself in Celtic sounds.

The accompanying sepia-toned video (by Godley & Creme), featuring Ure on acoustic guitar fronting The Chieftains, is emblematic of his post-Live Aid status. The visuals are painfully obvious, as men, women and children are zapped with a negative ray (like the extermination effect from *Doctor Who*'s Daleks), then fall to the ground in a pool of blood. The zoom-out revealing the pools that make up the shapes of the world's continents is nothing less than groan-inducing. If the acclaim and recognition Ure gained from Band Aid/Live Aid went to his head, it's a shame he didn't come up with better lyrics than 'If it's colour or creed or your old time religion/Well, fighting for that shows a pure lack of vision/The fight that we strive is the fight to survive/And we'll all fall down'.

As the album's second single – released on 9 November 1986 – it reached number 30: one better than 'Same Old Story'.

In the tour programme for 1986's *U-Vox* tour (the band's last before 2012), Ure stated:

> (Ultravox) have no barriers. We let a song and its arrangement dictate what that song should sound like. So a song like 'All Fall Down' was like you'd imagine a Jacques Brel Celtic protest song to sound. It has a very strong

Celtic folk feel, with acoustic guitars and instruments. We used Chieftains on it and went over to Dublin to record them. Although, at the time, the idea sounded really bizarre – the combination of us and them, a band who supposedly uses technology to its utmost, and this band who uses no technology at all. That combination works really well.

In 2012, Ure still thought highly of the song, though he regarded the overall *U-Vox* project as a failure. He told artrock.se: 'The album *U-Vox* is a mess and displays a band falling apart. But in 'All Fall Down', we successfully gather ourselves together with folk band The Chieftains in a very easy and powerful folk song'. Billed as Ultravox with The Chieftains, to many, the finished track sounds much more like The Chieftains with Midge Ure – perhaps the most unlike Ultravox track ever released under their name, until the 1990s, that is.

'Time To Kill' (Cross, Currie, Ure)
'Time To Kill' starts a trio of almost motivational songs. It opens with guitar and drums before becoming a more Ultravox-sounding track with a solid piano backing from Currie (at long last). It's a great side-two opener that could've easily suited *Quartet* or even *Lament*.

The frustration of commuting is captured in the opening couplet: 'Sitting on a train going 'round, 'round, get around/Looking at the same old places'. The chorus sums up the overall philosophy of grabbing the opportunities that cross our paths: 'Time for the taking/Turn it into something more than just/ Time to kill'. The almost spoken vocal middle section also hits home: 'Watch those minutes turn to hours/Watch those hours turn to days/Watch those days turn into years/Time to kill'. Overall, the lyric is a definite step up and an echo of past glories, but it's hardly as sophisticated as many of the songs on *Vienna* and *Rage In Eden*, and the band appear to be attempting rather bland late-1980s pop music in line with much else that was going on at the time.

It's an upbeat, positive song that's easy enough to like and enjoy, but like so much of *U-Vox*, it simply doesn't scream Ultravox. Whatever it was that had made the band's music special in the past had gone AWOL.

'Moon Madness' (Cross, Currie, Ure) 3:28
Like 'Time To Kill', this revives something akin to the classic Ultravox sound while pursuing a more positive lyric. It's the up-front nature of Currie's piano work and the strong guitar (presumably by Ure) that gives that flavour, while the vocal is also strong.

The opening verse suggests depression ('It drags me down'), followed by a chorus that outlines various fantasies, attributed to 'Moon madness again'. It's a companion piece to 'Time To Kill' as it plays to everyday frustrations, with another nod to the toils of commuters: 'Like strangers who nod on a station drag me down'. It may sound negative (and there's a lot that is bleak in nature), but 'Moon Madness' holds the possibility of redemption. Each of the fantasies has some hope of escape in them – riding on 'a snow white charger', escaping to 'a secret hideaway', somehow securing 'a million dollars'. The fantasies become less outlandish or unachievable, diminishing from the likes of 'a wild adventure' or sailing 'around the world' to the much-more-achievable 'Picture us with some happy moments'.

This and the previous track are the closest in sound that anything on *U-Vox* gets to traditional Ultravox (even 'Hiroshima Mon Amour' featured a sax solo!), yet these songs are like a fifth-generation photocopy of a photocopy.

'Follow Your Heart' (Cross, Currie, Ure) 4:53

The third of the positivity trilogy is a catchy track that can remain as an insistent earworm long after the first hearing. From the opening upbeat sounds, the song is difficult to dislike. In keeping with the two previous tracks, the message is firmly to 'Follow your own way'. There's a search for reassurance and direction: 'There must be something to rely on', 'There must be someone to depend on'. What's on offer has failed, from 'a thousand lies' to 'the preachings' and 'the gospel' (echoing 'Hymn'). Despite the upbeat positivity, these are rather banal observations and were rather commonplace at the time (The Thompson Twins had an album track of the same title in 1987 that wasn't a million miles removed from this track). It's not moody nor atmospheric in the way that a lot of Ultravox's earlier material was, but it is undeniably catchy and might've fared better in the 1986/1987 singles chart than the heavy-handed likes of 'All Fall Down' or 'All In One Day'.

'All In One Day' (Cross, Currie, Ure) 5:09

The pretension and obviousness of the 'All Fall Down' lyric returns with a vengeance. The result was the first Ultravox single to miss the top 40 since Midge Ure joined the band, with the well-meaning but dire 'All In One Day' slouching into the charts at a reprehensible number 88 (released on 8 June 1987). The era of Ultravox hits was well and truly over.

The subject matter was the Live Aid event, filtered through Ure's perception, confirming the strange place his involvement had left him in as a musical artist for the rest of the decade. Musically, 'All In One Day' was Currie's project. The band turned to *Quartet* producer George Martin to arrange the orchestra, with Martin also conducting. In the *U-Vox* tour programme, Ure said, 'We asked George Martin to arrange an orchestra for it. Billy did some stuff on it, but the rest of us just sat back and watched the orchestra play, which was quite nice, watching someone else perform it for you'.

It was to be the final Ultravox single. Perhaps it would've made for a cleaner finale to call it quits with 'Love's Great Adventure' and the success of the greatest hits album *The Collection*, which both did well in the charts.

Related Tracks

'3' (Cross, Currie, Ure) 4:01

Released as the B-side to 'Same Old Story', '3' is an instrumental where the title might be a reference to Ultravox minus Midge Ure. The percussion recalls some of Cann's old work, while the instrumentation recalls sounds last heard on *Quartet*'s B-sides and instrumentals. Currie then takes the glory with a delicious piano solo: the kind of instrumentation so much missed across much of *U-Vox*. Was this track (like 'Ukraine', see below) an early attempt by Cross and Currie (and perhaps a moonlighting Cann) to produce alternative material that might've featured on *U-Vox*? Ultimately, without further development, '3' is a slight doodle that really goes nowhere and eventually simply fades away.

'Dreams?' (Cross, Currie, Ure) 2:32

The B-side of 'All Fall Down' has echoes of Japan and Orchestral Manoeuvres in the Dark, quite unlike anything on the *U-Vox* album. Perhaps the work of Currie, it's a chance to play around with the kind of atmospheres and sounds that the Ultravox of old might've made use of but which were notable by their absence on *U-Vox*. The spoken extract – seemingly from a Radio 4 documentary about dreaming – offsets the (dreamy) sounds, and the entire thing might be related to the album track 'Dream On'.

'Stateless' (Cross, Currie, Ure) 2:51

Rhythmically interesting, at least, 'Stateless' was the B-side of 'All In One Day'. This had the makings of a finished song if only a lyric had been put to it. The no-doubt primary involvement of Currie on this experiment is clear, given some of the Visage-like sounds evident. There are more synth sounds used here than virtually anywhere on *U-Vox*. Once more, it's a B-side revealing a more interesting musical direction that could've been pursued if Ure hadn't been so dominant.

'Ukraine' (Cross, Currie) 3:24

A curiosity, this one: 1986-style Ultravox without Midge Ure. Produced by Cann, Currie and Cross, this ploughs rhythmic territory similar to 'All Fall Down', but is very different melodically. Currie cuts loose with his viola work across the top, while Cann keeps the ethnic rhythms going. Musically, it shows the kind of developments that might've brought the fans with them, rather than the overtly Ure-focused *U-Vox*. It was rejected as part of the *U-Vox* developmental work but saw release on the 1991 Billy Currie solo album *Stand Up And Walk*, which had all tracks by Currie, except 'Ukraine'. Currie wrote of this track on his website billycurrie.com:

> This track was actually intended for the Ultravox album. Warren Cann had control of the percussion and Chris Cross played the bass guitar. Conny

Plank produced the album. I used the English-made OSCar synth for the solo in the middle. This sound was devised specifically for me to replace the old ARP Odyssey sound that I had developed in Ultravox.

Revelation (1993)

Personnel:
Tony Fenelle: lead vocals, guitar
Billy Currie: violin, viola, keyboards, synthesizers
Gerry Laffy: guitar ('I Am Alive', 'No Turning Back')
Neal Wilkinson: drums ('I Am Alive', 'Perfecting The Art Of Common Ground')
Jackie Williams: backing vocals ('Revelation', 'Systems Of Love')
Richard Niles: conductor, string arrangements ('I Am Alive', 'The New Frontier')
Producers: Rod Gammons, Ultravox
Recorded at Master Rock, London; Berwick Street Studios, London
Label: DSB
Release date: 17 June 1993 (UK)
Chart places: -
Running time: 45:43

While the break-up of the most successful iteration of Ultravox might be blamed on Midge Ure's solo ambitions, he wasn't the only one to focus on their own work outside of the group structure prior to *U-Vox*. Warren Cann had worked with film composer Hans Zimmer in Helden – a project that also merged electronic, orchestral and classical influences. Chris Cross had worked with poet Maxwell Langdown and Ure on the left-field concept album *The Bloodied Sword* – about weapons and civilisation conflict in a vague fantasy setting. Billy Currie had been in Visage (with Ure) and had worked with Gary Numan back in 1979/1980, just prior to Ultravox's success. He'd always pursued his own largely private musical projects while channelling the bulk of his creative energies into Ultravox. During the band's 1985 hiatus, when Ure was involved in the Band Aid/Live Aid phenomenon and his nascent solo career, Currie was also pursuing other work, primarily as part of The Armoury Show. That band had formed in 1983 with the Skids' Richard Jobson on vocals. It also included guitarist John McGeoch, who'd been in Magazine and Siouxsie and the Banshees but had also worked with Currie as part of Visage, along with Jobson's Skids bandmate bass guitarist Russell Webb, who'd also been in Slik with Midge Ure. One-time Magazine drummer John Doyle was also involved. Currie became involved with their only studio album *Waiting For The Floods* (1985), playing violin on 'Higher Than The World', giving it something of an Ultravox flavour.

In the wake of the disintegration of Ultravox, Currie worked on two projects during 1988 – his first solo album *Transportation* and the Humania project with former Ultravox guitarist Robin Simon. (The Ultravox-like 1989 album *Sinews Of The Soul* wouldn't be released until 2005. It's far better than the 1990s Ultravox and worth seeking out.)

Currie wrote on his website: '(I) was ready to now do my own thing. I didn't just rush into it because I felt I first needed to make music with some musicians who had a different angle on things. This was in 1987, when

Ultravox had just disintegrated. I wrote and recorded three songs'. A second, more introspective solo album *Stand Up And Walk* followed in 1991, including the Currie/Cann/Cross track 'Ukraine', rejected from the *U-Vox* sessions.

Each of these solo albums had necessarily involved other musicians (Steve Howe, Toby Anderson, Kadir Guirey) or vocalists (Suzanne Bramson), pushing Currie back in the direction of resurrecting Ultravox in the early 1990s. (Some fans humorously refer to the 1970s band as UltraFoxx, the 1980s version as UreTravox, and the 1990s incarnation as CurrieVox.) Currie told *Music Technology* magazine in March 1993: 'When I started thinking about putting a new Ultravox together, I began looking for a good production deal'. That led him to Berwick Street Studios, where producer Rod Gammons had been churning out hits for the likes of The Shamen, East 17 and The Orb. Gammons had been working with Birmingham-born singer/guitarist Tony Fenelle for about 18 months when Currie arrived looking to develop a more 1990s and possibly dance-oriented Ultravox. Gammons put Currie and Fenelle together, and the foundation of the new band was established. Talking to *Music Technology*, Gammons said: 'The songs are more important than the token inclusion of hip effects just to please a few specialist DJs. You can make a record sound *now* for about six months, and then it soon becomes last year's record. I want people to be able to put this album on in three years' time or ten years' time and say, 'Yeah, this still sounds pretty classic''.

Replacing the likes of John Foxx and especially Midge Ure was no easy task for Currie. His relationship with Fenelle developed as they worked with Gammons on the songs. Fenelle noted: 'We got to know each other as we worked. That was harder than actually recording because we had no way of knowing exactly which way the other would go. When you've rehearsed with a band for years, you'll know where you're all going ... we literally spent months learning about each other'.

The first product of these efforts was the rather ill-advised 'Vienna 92' single (released only in Germany) of April 1992, with the cheekily titled 'Systems Of Love' on the B-side (which ultimately found a place on *Revelation*). All the revised take on 'Vienna' proved was that Fenelle was no Midge Ure. Even worse was the abominable 'Goodnight Vienna' dance mix. There was enough of an echo of the original Ultravox sound on 'Systems Of Love' to attract some Ultravox fans, even if Fenelle's stadium-rock-oriented vocal style was unsuitable.

A second single – 'I Am Alive' (again with 'Systems Of Love' on the B-side) – presaged the release of *Revelation*. Currie explained the thinking behind this sample-and-see approach: 'You can step back after one track, listen to it, and think about the next step.'

The few *Revelation* reviews that appeared were not particularly kind. (For the most part, the album was ignored.) Chris Welsh wrote in *Rock World*:

Billy Currie works hard to revive the original spirit of Ultravox, with new singer Tony Fenelle replacing the errant Midge Ure. Tony has a nice voice, but it will be quite a task to convince the masses at large that this is the new Ultravox. Well, it *is* the new Ultravox, but will songs like 'I Am Alive' pitch the project back into the charts and onto the radio? That will be the crucial test. Meanwhile, there is no mistaking the chiming chords, the bright-eyed optimistic vocals and the wide-screen melodies, hot on drama and rich in orchestration. Tony sings up a storm on *Revelation*, but there are moments of pause and indecision that are quite puzzling. Nevertheless, there are some good songs here, and we wish 'em well.

That was about as positive as it got, with a meagre four out of ten rating from *Rock World*.

In *Q* magazine, Jim White went even lower, with just one out of five:

Shorn of his old chum and inspiration Midge Ure, Billy Currie has had to go some way to find someone, anyone, to sign up for his latest incarnation of the long-forgotten and hardly-missed Ultravox. He fetched up in Berlin and the old East German state record company, now in private hands. Currie took with him a George Michael look-alike singer Tony Fenelle and a fist of co-written songs with titles like 'Systems Of Love' and 'Perfecting The Art Of Common Ground', which are presumably the sort of thing which pass as current in the old East. The result is depressingly one-paced – ten epic pomp rockers full of grandiose keyboard chords and portentous lyrics. Fenelle pitches his voice close to *Heroes*-vintage David Bowie, which may be a fashionable place to camp these days, but simply pronouncing 'revelation' as 'revelayshone' is not enough.

In a 2023 album-by-album survey, *Classic Pop* said of *Revelation*: 'Whereas the band were once considered pioneers, their ninth LP sounded hopelessly dated. 'No Turning Back' and 'Unified' both strive for anthemic status but end up resembling failed A Song For Europe entries, while 'I Am Alive' is the kind of fist-pumping schlock you could imagine David Hasselhoff belting out on a crane above the fallen Berlin Wall'.

Currie was interviewed about the new Ultravox in *Replay* magazine:

I saw Midge a couple of years ago. Midge had no objections to my plans, and when I saw Warren Cann, he didn't mind either. In fact, Warren said he'd like to be in the lineup, but wanted to play guitar rather than drums, which was the reason he left Ultravox in the first place. Chris Cross, who'd been the original bass and synthesizer player, avoided my phone calls for a fortnight and then ... even hinted that he might like to play on the follow-up album. To be honest, I think that there is still a niche for Ultravox's kind of music, and I hope people who liked the earlier records will like the new stuff. Over the years there have been other bands who have tried to copy the Ultravox sound, but they've never quite got it right. That's why it's now a good time for the band to return.

On keeping the Ultravox name, Currie admitted it was hard to let it go: 'It's so much a part of my life. I've put everything into it, and it's still not finished'.

'I Am Alive' (Currie, Fenelle, Gammons) 4:56
Currie's piano is very much to the fore at the beginning and end of 'I Am Alive', but the biggest shock comes with the arrival of Tony Fenelle's vocals – a very slick mid-1990s approach that doesn't live up to the Foxx or Ure-era Ultravox but would work fine on a cruise ship or in a Las Vegas residency. The song features such trite chorus lines as 'I am alive/I am who I want to be' and 'I am alive/And this is my destiny'. Cheekily, such lines as 'passing strangers' and 'artificial life' echo (deliberately or not) past Ultravox glories. It's slick MOR rock that might've found more appeal in the US market than in the always-fussy UK music scene.

The single found favour nowhere, failing to chart. The most interesting bit comes right at the end after Fenelle's vocals have (thankfully) faded away and Currie gets to play around with his instruments. More of that would be very welcome. Said Fenelle of the recording: 'The first songs we wrote together are the ones that people like most. 'I Am Alive' was the first one we wrote, and that's the first single. I came in from New York, and three days later, there was the song. We really fell into it naturally'.

'Revelation' (Currie, Fenelle, Gammons) 4:06
In a similar vein, 'Revelation' kicks off with piano, but at a slower tempo than 'I Am Alive'. It sounds like Christian rock, from the lyrics to the bland yet functional musicality. It's a big sound, but ultimately forgettable. 'Revelation' sounds positive lyrically, suggesting there's a future for humanity beyond 'politically motivated total mind control' if you'd only 'open your eyes to the revelation'. Whether Currie was aware or not, the religious implications can't be ignored.

Just like the previous track, things get interesting when the vocals disappear and Currie gets to strut his stuff. Fenelle was clear on the approach he, Currie and Gammons wanted, and it was to be a dramatic break from the past: 'We were interested in a big sound. My thinking was to have hard rock drums rather than machine-like ticks. Different from the early Ultravox stuff. So it was a departure for Billy. Plus, it's not the old Ultravox; it's a brand-new Ultravox. When I arrived I wasn't going to wear tapered sideburns and a pencil moustache. Billy's the main man and always has been. He's the keyboard player that put that stamp on the band from day one. It wasn't going to lose that'.

'Systems Of Love' (Currie, Fenelle, Gammons) 4:32

Released twice as a single B-side, 'Systems Of Love' was the track some fans saw as having hope of Currie's new incarnation going some way to recapturing past glories. The title alone was a cheeky riff on the Foxx-era album title *Systems Of Romance*.

Distorted guitar raises hopes for something like the tracks on *Vienna* before the stuttered dance rhythm appears, causing hearts to sink. Fenelle offers a stronger, less cheesy vocal here, suggesting that early on, he and Currie may have been more focused on echoing the Ultravox sound. The catchy chorus is equal to much on *U-Vox*, with the female backing vocals recalling that album and some of the tracks on *Lament*. However, there are enough tacky 1990s sounds to make it fail the test. Three minutes in, a trademark Currie synth line suddenly appears, harking back to the pre-*Quartet* era, but it's all too short-lived to make an impact.

There are yet more hints of Christian rock in the breakout verse: 'Be my disciple/All I ask is put your faith in me/There's a better way, you know it/Don't be afraid of divine technology'. On the vocal approach, Currie was clear he wasn't going to impose anything on Fenelle: 'I didn't want to [tie] Tony to my style; that would have been wrong. You've got to create something new'.

'Perfecting The Art Of Common Ground' (Currie, Fenelle, Laffy) 5:17

Slower and more contemplative, this initially sounds like it might be going for the 'Vienna' or 'Visions In Blue' vibe. Musically, it could've easily been an old B-side, but the vocals again let things down. Fenelle's big-is-always-better approach overshadows everything good Currie might be accomplishing. Oddly, bits of the piano part seem to anticipate the theme of TV show *The X-Files*, which began in 1993.

Later on, Currie finds his moment to soar, making the sections without the intrusive vocals far better. Despite these welcome flourishes, the track can't escape the blandness that suffuses so much of this album. Ever-ambitious and interested in his music, Currie was happy to cleverly recall some of the past Ultravox glories within this new incarnation: 'There's one loop under a slide guitar solo on 'Perfecting The Art Of Common Ground' which is taken from an early-'70s heavy-rock vibe. I won't tell you what it is, but it just comes through perfectly. I'm playing games with Ultravox's history a bit – I'd zoom in on this middle section with the slide guitar ... and it's real *Rage In Eden* period, about 1981, offset by this particular loop, so, using technology to make quite subtle statements'.

'The Great Outdoors' (Currie, Fenelle) 4:12

At this stage of *Revelation*, what primarily comes across is the sameness of the tracks. There's yet more of Fenelle's competent-yet-strangely-lacklustre vocal, playing out over an intriguing opening salvo that quickly degenerates into the same old overwrought stuff. There are the merest hints of Currie's classic piano and violin work peeking through the noise here, but it's simply not enough to compensate for the karaoke vocal style. To give him his due, Tony Fenelle sticks to his guns, delivering a consistent sound, but it's so unlike anything previously released under the Ultravox name that questions have to be asked of Currie about what he was thinking. After about three minutes, a nice instrumental section suggests what could've been from this Ultravox revival if it hadn't been so sunk by the vocals.

The song itself is full of bland lyrical pablum about standing out from the crowd, letting moments pass us by, and falling through the hands of time, but there's nothing imaginative about any of this. The bland competency is almost offensive.

'The Closer I Get To You' (Currie, Fenelle) 4:13
Nothing sounds more dated than music trying to be on-trend with its times. Here, Fenelle varies his vocal delivery, but the pseudo-rap comes across as none-more-1990s. The lyrics are a word salad (but not in the intriguing John Foxx style), while the music is driven by indifferent percussion, overwrought guitars and an attempt at pseudo-dance music. The central musical breakdown is halfway interesting, but again, it entirely dates the track. The great shame is that the branch of 1990s music that this take on Ultravox aligned itself with was the bland mainstream rather than the more interesting experimental edges. One thing the two previous incarnations of Ultravox prided themselves on (certainly through to *Rage In Eden*, but also including some of the material on *Lament*) was their desire to try something new, to push their music into unfamiliar shapes. The problem with *Revelation* is telling one track from the next as it descends track by track into an undifferentiated muzak sludge. For a pseudo-love song, 'The Closer I Get to You' lacks any passion or desire, with terrible lines like, 'Pure emotion/ You can't conceal/We touch, we come alive/We'll know that this time it's for real'. Even the worst of the much-maligned *U-Vox* doesn't seem so bad in comparison.

'No Turning Back' (Currie, Fenelle) 4:21
More than anything else, the music of *Revelation* takes aim at a kind of 1990s stadium rock sound yet manages to miss it by a mile. Currie's piano-playing features here, but the parts are so simple as to be unobtrusive. Fenelle belts out the vocal as if he's trying to reach the back row of a particularly huge venue, but that simply doesn't work on an album of recorded music.

This one's the opposite of 'The Closer I Get To You', as it's evidently a break-up song: 'I hate to leave/But there's no turning back/You may think that I'm wrong/But hear what I'm saying'. A middle-section guitar break attempts to imitate Ry Cooder (badly). What this stuff really needed was a big, bold brass section (calling *U-Vox*!).

Love songs were never a big part of the Ultravox repertoire, and their preponderance on *Revelation* suggests a lack of imagination on the part of all involved. Ure may have objected to Cann having written so many of the lyrics on *Vienna* and *Rage In Eden*, but his offbeat take on songwriting was what gave Ultravox its edge over all those other early-1980s new wave, New Romantic and electropop outfits. That, combined with the experimental music, gave Ultravox a unique sound that *Revelation* is almost completely devoid of.

'True Believer' (Currie, Fenelle, Gammons) 4:56
There's a sudden, unexpected blast of interest as 'True Believer' opens with the tuning of a radio. It's a welcome break from the bland run of songs that have all sounded the same and recalls some of the sonic trickery that was so central to *Rage In Eden*, particularly recalling the opening of 'I Remember (Death In The Afternoon)'. The audio clip of a radio (or television) evangelist (possibly Kenneth Copeland) suggests a lyric that might take issue with religion as a money-making scheme. The problem is that the lyric can play both ways, tearing down or reinforcing evangelical Christianity, especially on the evidence of earlier tracks like 'Revelation'. Do these lines attack or *support* Christianity?:

> Got to be a true believer
> Burning up inside with fever
> One with God
> You've got to pay for your devotion
> Feel a little true emotion
> One with God

It can be read either way.
At least Fenelle takes a different approach on the vocal, and some of the music track suggests a freshness from Currie and co., yet it's not a patch on anything that might be considered the *real* Ultravox. The only times they used such media clips, as heard here, were on B-sides such as 'Dreams?'. Even the best on *Revelation* is worse than the worst-ever Ultravox B-side. Come back 'Break Your Back' – all is forgiven!

'Unified' (Currie, Fenelle) 4:27
With hopes raised by the slight difference offered in 'True Believer', the penultimate track crashes back down to Earth with more of the same old stuff that makes up the rest of *Revelation*. There's a bright, upbeat pop sound about much of this stuff, but it's so undistinguished, layered in dated 1990s sounds and buried under Fenelle's dominating and bland vocals that it simply fails to stick.
Again, the lyric is built from religious references – 'exaltation', 'devotion', 'destiny' and being 'sanctified'. There's a vague Spanish lilt to Currie's

keyboards and the guitar work this time, but it's quickly lost, buried under the wall-of-sound production and Fenelle's vocal. The only *Revelation* here is that this band sounds nothing like Ultravox!

'The New Frontier' (Currie, Fenelle, Gammons) 4:43
The final track saw a welcome return of Currie's strings, but it really was an example of too-little-far-too-late. This slower, more contemplative track is (yet again) undone by Fenelle's all-encompassing singing. There's more lyrical nonsense – being 'guided by the light', 'a destiny unfolds', the need to 'rise again' and even 'testify', suggesting yet more Christian rock.

It all peters out a little inoffensively – the final entry in ten missed opportunities. If nothing else, *Revelation* simply proved that Currie alone was not enough to recreate the magic that made up Ultravox. Without Cann, the band had lost some of that magic when it came to 1986's *U-Vox*, but with no Cross, no Foxx and no Ure, there wasn't much left for Currie to conjure with.

Talking to Adam Locks at beatmag.net in 2006, Billy Currie looked back at the ill-fated *Revelation*: 'I think some of the *Revelation* album is absolute crap. It was difficult to try and do something new with a singer ... this terrible soft soul crept in there. I do quite like 'Perfecting The Art Of Common Ground'. I started writing lyrics on *Revelation* and *Ingenuity*. It was something I had to do ... It wasn't a good idea, but, in retrospect, it's always easy to say that'.

Ingenuity (1994)

Personnel:
Sam Blue: lead vocals
Billy Currie: viola, keyboards, synthesizers
Vinny Burns: guitar
Tony Holmes: drums
Gary Williams: bass
Producers: Billy Currie, Charlie Francis
Recorded at The Stone Room, London
Label: Resurgence/Intercord (Germany)
Release date: 10 November 1994 (UK)
Chart places: -
Running time: 44:48

The failure of *Revelation* – critically and creatively – to make any kind of impact, either on Ultravox fans or beyond in the wider music business, did not deter Billy Currie from his mission to take Ultravox through the 1990s. Talking to Ultravox fanzine *Extreme Voice* #14, he explained: 'We still had some gigs to do when Tony Fenelle left the band'. To that end, Currie had to put a band together and find a new vocalist to fulfil those contractual obligations: 'I kept with Tony (Holmes) the drummer because I thought he was good ... I started auditioning, and Tony brought this friend of his Gary Williams along ... You've got to be really careful after you've met someone like Tony Fenelle, 'cause they can seem okay on the front, but Gary Williams did seem alright ... I'd got the three of us straight away and I started rehearsing ... I met-up with Vinny Burns down in rehearsals, and the band seemed to work really well together'. Finding a new vocalist proved to be more problematic:

I tried one guy who had been in ELO Part 2 and had a great voice but had listened to *Revelation* too much and had copied Tony's voice – it was very similar, that kind of middle-of-the-road sort of AOR sound. He was very good though ... I wasn't going to do what I did with Tony Fenelle, like 'Right, let's do it', that kind of impulsive decision ... It was a very strange time for me, as you can imagine; it was like Tony Fenelle had really given me a good kick in the head ... Sam (Blue) came in and I quite warmed to him. I think it's hearing a Geordie accent instead of constantly hearing Londoners. Not being a Londoner myself, I related to him ... he'd just got a very good voice ... he'd got real clarity in his high frequencies, and that was really nice. It was something that could relate to the slight classical orientation that still comes through in the music. He'd got a real power as well.

Prior to entering the studio, Currie developed many of the tracks that would make up *Ingenuity,* working with his keyboards in his back room at home. Then, he brought in Sam Blue to work through the material, further developing it from a vocal point of view. Throughout the 1980s, Blue had worked with a variety of bands, such as Emerson, LA Secrets, Ya Ya and Empire. He essentially co-wrote the *Ingenuity* album with Currie and guitarist Vinny Burns, although, in the traditional post-John Foxx Ultravox tradition, the credits (and hence the income) were split equally among the five members. Three of the initial tracks completed were 'The Silent Cries', 'There Goes A Beautiful World' and the instrumental 'Majestic' which ultimately closed the album.

Currie took technology and human achievement as themes for the album, telling *Extreme Voice* #14: 'Things today are just amazing when compared to what it was like 15 years ago. We were involved with technology, just [as] in the 1970s.'

Ingenuity was put together in Currie's studio in downtime.

It was recorded in patches. We'd go in and do two days, and then go in and do a week ... (Vinny Burns) had six days to do his guitar, which is a fair luxury, really, but he's a good guitarist and I wanted it right ... When I did the keyboards, I took about a week, which, when you think that for the most expensive album we ever did – *Quartet* – we put all the stuff down in four weeks at Air Studios and then spent two months in Montserrat ... The actual mixing (on *Ingenuity*) took exactly two weeks at the Roundhouse Studio ... We did *Systems Of Romance* in two weeks, and we did *Vienna* in three weeks!

The different approach paid dividends, resulting in an album that – though not quite capturing the classic Ultravox sound (though it gets close in some isolated moments) – was a dramatic step up from the material on *Revelation*. As a singer, Sam Blue was a more-than-adequate Ure replacement, offering a more sympathetic approach than Fenelle had and giving Currie enough space for the music to also stand out. There is more variety across the tracks, with Currie keeping tight control of the process, mixing other's contributions in a more positive way. Overall, the result is listenable, but it still doesn't deserve to exist under the Ultravox banner.

Certainly, the fanzine *Extreme Voice* was impressed at the time:

Ingenuity is a very *instant* album, much more so than *Revelation*. It's been a firm favourite of ours since we first heard, and we've not felt so strongly about an Ultravox album since *Lament*. Gone are the semi-dance beats; Billy's violin work is as soaringly magnificent as when John Foxx was in the band. As for 'There Goes A Beautiful World', we weren't sure about the crowd noise at first, but now it seems completely appropriate. One of the most notable tracks is 'Majestic', which is an instrumental, and the first to appear exclusively on an Ultravox album since 1981's 'The Ascent' and believe us when we say that it was worth the wait. Our only criticism of it is that it's not long enough!

Fans had been starved of decent Ultravox output since 1986's *U-Vox* – diehards might claim since 1984's *Lament*. It was understandable then that the dramatic improvement in sound between the disastrous *Revelation* and the passable *Ingenuity* could've seemed like a near-return to former glory. In the cold light of day, over 25 years later, it's clearer than ever before that the only ones who could come close to replicating the sound of 1980s Ultravox would be that era's lineup. It was to take another two decades, almost, but they would be 'like pictures that come back again' – to quote the single-best Ultravox song: *Rage In Eden*'s 'We Stand Alone'.

'Ingenuity' (Blue, Burns, Currie, Holmes, Williams) 4:44
Opening track 'Ingenuity' immediately feels different to just about everything on *Revelation*. There's a pulsing rhythm and synth line (from a Korg, giving this new Ultravox a different-yet-familiar feel) like a 1980s throwback, with Currie finally reintroducing his pitch-bending approach to synth instrumentation. Far more than on the previous album, this – musically at least – feels like it could be a potential Ultravox successor.

On the vocal front, Sam Blue is closer to Ure in his warmer, more restrained tone than Fenelle. There's a theme to the song, too, made clear by the opening lines: 'Reach for the stars/The space race/Man on the moon'. The song makes a call for 'Ingenuity right now' – a return to the kind of scientific achievement realised by the 1960s space race in the face of a late-20th-century society that was failing. Currie admitted to the space theme, but despite repeated space iconography elsewhere, he claimed it was 'just for the title track, not a theme throughout the album. That song 'Ingenuity' is all about the space race and where we've got to so far, and it's a little bit like an implication that it was all done for political ends and that we haven't got anywhere really, and that's why the spaceman on the front looks a little bit pathetic. The word 'ingenuity' describes the human race and what we've achieved'.

A pulsing guitar interlude is welcome, along with some teasing backing vocals. The merest hints of that trademark Ultravox sound make this better than anything on *Revelation*, but it's still a bit too safe and a bit too bland (and redolent of its 1990s origins) to be truly part of the overall canon.

'There Goes A Beautiful World' (Blue, Burns, Currie, Holmes, Williams) 4:10
Drums and synths open this lyrically simple dance song, and it wouldn't be too much of a stretch to imagine Midge Ure singing it. A strong guitar line runs throughout, that even culminates in the sound of a celebratory crowd. Currie admitted, 'That's from a sample. We were having a lot of fun remixing it. That has been through a hell of a lot of changes.'

The lyric is hardly complex, but there is something to be said for simplicity. There's something of the old, abstract Ultravox lyrics in the chorus: 'Oh, the circumstances detailed/The force of the run/Oh, the messages unfold/ There goes a beautiful world'. There's still too much 1990s production and too many dated sounds (not something that can be said of *Rage In Eden*, for example). The machine rhythms are too programmed and the bubbling synth line and handclap effects are too regular. About two and a half minutes in, there's a nice guitar flourish and a hint of Currie's keyboards. Despite all that, this could be a track from any run-of-the-mill mid-1990s band.

'Give It All Back' (Blue, Burns, Currie, Holmes, Williams) 4:21
Slowing the pace, Currie's viola makes an appearance over a basic rock mid-tempo ballad. Stabbing guitars and staccato vocals help give life to the track after a somnambulistic start. The regular tempo changes liven things up, but it's all a bit too Marillion. Halfway through, the viola erupts, offering a vague *Rage In Eden* feel – something the 1990s Ultravox should've featured more heavily. All too soon, it reverts to grinding rock, with the viola struggling to hold attention. As with 'There Goes A Beautiful World', there's much more to this than anything on *Revelation*, but it's still the merest distant echo of former glories.

'Future Picture Forever' (Blue, Burns, Currie, Holmes, Williams) 4:17
The viola continues its resurgence on another slower track that's supported by a decent melody. From the opening, this sounds like an Ultravox B-side until the dreamy vocal kicks in, which pushes things in a different direction. Over the guitar and piano, Blue does his best Ure impression (especially on the chorus), with the vocal echoes helping things along.

There are also echoes of some of John Foxx's old lyrical concerns, in lines like: 'If I could see the future/And I would tear up the picture/The future picture forever'.

The big guitar solo halfway through is a bit generic, and it builds to a grand rock finale that's also very obvious. Sometimes – to their own detriment in the 1980s – if there was one thing that Ultravox tried to avoid, it was anything too easy or too obvious.

'The Silent Cries' (Blue, Burns, Currie, Holmes, Williams) 4:14
Rhythmically, there was nothing on *Revelation* – or *Ingenuity* to this point – that could rival the urgency of classics like 'The Thin Wall' or 'All Stood Still'. Warren Cann's experiments with live drumming and programmable machines on *Lament* were long in the past. 'The Silent Cries' gets close, even recalling some of the Foxx-era classics in its guitar work. It certainly feels familiar enough until Blue's falsetto kicks in. This was a register that Ure used occasionally but which never really suited the band. Its return here spoils what otherwise might've been a triumphant track. There's some

synth noodling, harking back to Currie's past glories. The chorus – even if its banter about 'spades' makes little sense – is at least catchy and memorable. After three minutes, Currie lets loose in a way that could almost convince you that this is the real deal... almost.

'Distance' (Blue, Burns, Currie, Holmes, Williams) 3:51

Unexpected variations in tempo were always an Ultravox thing, so a track that starts slow, speeds up considerably for the middle section and then returns to a slower tempo for the climax was another welcome development on *Ingenuity*. The chorus is nice – 'Won't distance you/Don't want resistance to/Looks like I distanced you' – with the stretched-out final 'yooouuu' recalling the best of Ure's vocals. A central guitar riff livens things up again, and the overall structure gives 'Distance' a welcome familiarity. The musical collapse just before the final slow-down is a nice touch, too. Like the previous track, this also comes to a definitive end rather than simply fading.

Unlike most of *Revelation*, this fits nicely among a group of much more memorable songs where the variety of approaches at least makes it easier for the listener to tell one track from another and perhaps more easily associate the music with the song titles. Basic stuff, sure, but welcome.

'Ideals' (Blue, Burns, Currie, Holmes, Williams) 4:12

The guitar is once more to the fore here, but Currie offers strong piano support while Tony Holmes pounds away consistently on the drums. The mix of elements plays out well, driving the track along and allowing Blue's questioning vocal its own space to spread. There's almost something hypnotic about how it unfolds and something Thin Lizzy-like about Vinny Burns' later guitar licks. Perhaps the band were asking for it with a line like 'The magic has lost its appeal' because try as they might – and while this second 1990s lineup is a huge advance on the Fenelle-fronted incarnation – it's still an impossible task to recapture what made Ultravox so good in the 1980s. Even when the lineup from that period reconvened – initially only to play *the hits* live – they couldn't resist giving another final album a go. As *Brilliant* revealed, though it came the closest, even that couldn't exactly replicate the sound they'd previously achieved, thanks to changes in technology and the one thing no one can escape: time.

'Who'll Save You'(Blue, Burns, Currie, Holmes, Williams) 6:36

The longest track on *Ingenuity*, 'Who'll Save You' opens with a pleasing instrumental stretch that recalls some of the 1980s classics, even if it sounds a bit more Gary Numan than Ultravox. It's good to have 90 seconds of musical grace before the vocal arrives. It's about the first time Gary Williams' bass-playing makes itself felt in any great measure, while Blue stretches himself vocally to offer another variation on his Ure take, where Tony Fenelle stuck resolutely to his one-tone stadium-rock approach. Where a nice Currie sweeping synth solo might've sat – right in the middle of the song – we simply get more guitar work from Vinny Burns. It's not bad, but a wider range of sounds – especially from Currie – would've worked much better in these stretches between the vocals. The last minute or so returns to the instrumental opening, with strains of some old *Rage In Eden*-era sounds sneaking in: just a wee bit too late overall.

'A Way Out, A Way Through' (Blue, Burns, Currie, Holmes, Williams) 4:07
The bass – this time a sequenced synth bass – is to the fore again. The final vocal track on *Ingenuity* opens with a classic Ultravox drum stab and guitar riff before turning a bit soft. Burns offers up a guitar riff that could be from 'New Europeans', while Currie's piano aims for 'Vienna' majesty, but the combination all falls some way short. Halfway through, Currie's synths kick in big-time, bringing a smile to anyone familiar with the band's 1980s output. For whatever reason, Currie chose to use such signature moments sparingly across *Revelation* and *Ingenuity*, presumably for fear of turning the new Ultravox into a 1980s tribute band – which is almost exactly what that 1980s lineup was to become in the 2010s.

'Majestic' (Blue, Burns, Currie, Holmes, Williams) 4:18
The suitably titled 'Majestic' is a glorious instrumental that closes *Ingenuity* in the way that 'Astradyne' opened *Vienna*. Though credited to the whole band, it's clearly the work of Billy Currie and plays out like a track from one of his solo instrumental albums, given something of an Ultravox kick. Looking forward to further Ultravox-branded output, Currie was optimistic: 'I'd like to do more instrumentals on the next one 'cause I think you do start to feel like you're just doing a song formula. I tried to get out of the song formula on some tracks, but I think when we do manage to do another album, I'd like to get two or three instrumentals on it'. Quite how more instrumentals on an Ultravox album would be different from instrumentals on a Currie solo effort, wasn't clear. He could obviously do whatever he wanted on that score, especially if it didn't involve others.

'Majestic' is the most Ultravox-like track across both of these 1990s albums and is all the better for not having vocals forced on it from Fenelle or Blue. At just over four minutes in length, if anything, 'Majestic' is simply too short (just as *Extreme Voice* suggested) and could've easily extended to the seven-minute length of 'Astradyne' without outstaying its welcome.

This was the last track recorded for the album, and it turned out to be a great one to go out on.

Brilliant (2012)

Personnel:
Midge Ure: lead vocals, guitar, synthesizers
Billy Currie: violin, keyboards, synthesizers, piano
Chris Cross: bass, synthesizers
Warren Cann: drums
Producers: Stephen Lipson, Ultravox
Recorded at The Lakehouse, Montreal, Canada; Environment, Bath, UK; Sarm West, London, UK; Battery, London, UK; Studio City Sound, Los Angeles, US
Label: Chrysalis
Release date: 25 May 2012 (UK)
Charts: UK: 21, AU: 59, BEL: 182, CZH: 42, GER: 27, IT: 84, PO: 28, SC: 13, SWE: 36, SWI: 67
Running time: 52:48

Fifteen years after 1994's *Ingenuity*, the seemingly impossible (or at least the highly unlikely) happened – the classic 1980s Ultravox lineup reunited, initially for a 2009/2010 *Nostalgia* tour. However, thoughts soon turned to the possibility of recording new music. That led to 2012's perhaps arrogantly titled *Brilliant*: the final Ultravox album (to date, over a decade later).

It was something few saw coming – not most of the fans and certainly not most of the band members. The 2009 reunion came on the anniversary of the assembly of the second Ultravox lineup. Speaking to rememberingtheeighties. com in 2009, Midge Ure explained: 'It started from the fact that it was 30 years since we wrote 'Vienna', which made it a celebratory thing. If we were going to do anything on a musical level ever again, then this would be the year to do it, and that's what got us all talking and contemplating the idea'. The reunion had its awkward moments, largely thanks to Warren Cann having been fired prior to 1986's heavily criticised *U-Vox*, but partly due to Billy Currie's unsuccessful attempts to revive the Ultravox brand in the early 1990s. Ure admitted, 'I'd not spoken to Warren in 23 years. He's lived in Los Angeles for most of that time. I'd been in touch with Chris a few times, and Billy and I had spoken, but never about this. It was always just about generalities or technical things about contractual nonsense, but not in any positive musical sense. It was never planned, never even thought of. Of course, people ask you all the time whether you would, but everyone just sort of avoided the issue'.

It was the band's former manager Chris O'Donnell who approached each band member individually but simultaneously. He'd noted the September 2008 remastered re-releases of *Vienna* and *Rage In Eden* with additional material and the fact that Ure and Currie had already reunited (also in 2008) at Abbey Road to play an acoustic version of 'Vienna' for Absolute Radio's *Geoff Lloyd Show*. O'Donnell – then working for concert promoter Live Nation – saw the possibilities of a lucrative reunion tour if only the fractious members could bury their past differences.

When asked to play 'Vienna' live, Ure made the first move in putting the band back together: 'They had asked me to go do some radio promo when (the remastered) *Vienna* came out ... asked me if I fancied doing something live. So I phoned Billy up and asked him to come play on the piano, and that was it. As soon as we did that, the websites just crashed and people went crazy that we were in the same room, not only talking but playing. That made us realise it wasn't the horror we thought it was going to be! It was easy'.

Currie was initially reluctant, despite (or perhaps because of) his previous attempts to keep the Ultravox brand fresh, but Cross and Ure, on a visit to Currie's home, helped persuade him to come onboard. At rememberingtheeighties.com, Currie noted: 'My immediate thought was 'Yikes! I'm not sure about this'. Then I realised, why not? Let's move things on. There had been talk of the tour at that point, but we hadn't actually decided to do it'. Warren Cann flew to London from L.A. in March, agreed to join the revival, and the band set about arranging rehearsal time. Any worry about reconnecting after many years evaporated once all four were in the same room. There was a collective decision made by all involved to forget the past in order to focus on the present.

On 6 November 2008, it was officially announced that Ultravox had reformed and would be starting the 15-date *Return To Eden* UK tour at the Edinburgh Playhouse on 10 April 2009 – the first time this lineup had performed live since their Live Aid date in 1985. Talking to the *Sunday Mail*, Ure was at pains to point out that this tour would be a one-off event: 'We're not trying to recapture our youth and won't be writing new songs or recording another album. This is about celebrating our music and our anniversary'.

In February 2009, the remastered CD releases continued with *Quartet* and *Lament*. The UK dates proved to be so successful that the band extended the tour to Europe, adding dates in Germany and Belgium. A live CD/DVD of their sold-out gig at London's Roundhouse was released in April 2010. That year also saw the *one-off* tour extended with *Return To Eden II*, which took the band across Europe again.

It was during this second bout of touring that thoughts turned seriously to recording new material: something they'd initially declared they had no interest in. Ure addressed the issue when talking to *Release* magazine in 2012:

We rediscovered ourselves; we realised that we were actually quite a good band. It wasn't all about the synthesizers and it wasn't about what everyone had written for the past 15 years. I am a guitarist first and foremost, and it was great to see Billy with the violins, so that appears on the record. We dug out his old ARP Odyssey synthesizer for some of the solos. We were inspired, I think, by that tour. We are a rock band and a very powerful one. It is a very powerful sound that we make. We tried to take some of the energy that we got from the tour and put that into new recordings.

Nevertheless, there was some trepidation about writing and recording again in a very different 21st-century environment. The trio of Ure, Currie and Cross got together at Ure's residential studio in Canada for the recording. Ure noted: 'Warren had commitments in Los Angeles, and he didn't have to be part of it until later. It is quite a dangerous thing to do because, in that kind of tense environment, things could have easily gone horribly wrong. We were in the middle of the woods, in a cabin by the lake. It was freezing cold and there was no one there to talk to other than the band. But it worked out brilliantly, mainly because we got along so well and the creativity was there'.

The album spent just one week in the UK charts but hit a respectable 21 – not bad after 28 years away. It didn't exhibit staying power, however, and quickly vanished.

The reviews were mixed, with many welcoming the return of the band to live performing three decades after *Vienna* but not being so positive about the new recordings. Theartsdesk.com claimed, '*Brilliant* is as good as anything Ultravox have ever done. If you liked their early-1980s prime, you'll love this. The fabulously doomy robot ballad 'Fall', the monstrous stadium anthem 'Satellite', the vaguely Human League-ish 'Change': well, every song, really. They haven't changed a jot. If anything, age and a 28-year break have made them more sternly soaring, more essence-of-Ultravox'.

Louder's take was more nuanced:

(Ultravox) are making a fine noise indeed ... Their chilling dystopian visions may have thawed somewhat, but there is no denying the imperious splendour of the title track or the jackhammer pulse of 'Rise' ... Midge Ure still sings as though delivering sermons from the mount, there is an air of pomp throughout *Brilliant* and the band tend to belabour every melody. But then, if they didn't do that, they wouldn't be Ultravox, would they?

However, the website godisinthetvzine.co.uk declared *Brilliant* their 'bummer album of the week', noting, 'It's called *Brilliant*, and let me assure you it most certainly is not. Every track is a pretentious one-word title and contains predictable plinky-plonk keyboards, ending up with a bunch of songs that wouldn't even have been credible B-sides back then'.

Somewhere in the middle came consequence.net: '(Ultravox) revisits the unapologetically huge synth-rock sound that the band was so successful with between 1980 and 1986. Within the first minute of *Brilliant*, the sky-scraping anthems, the pulsing synth lines and the gorgeous textures of 'Live' immediately evoke the band's *Vienna/Rage In Eden* era ... Contained within that song is pretty much any reason one would have to pay attention to an Ultravox album in 2012'.

Brilliant brought Ultravox's chart history to a conclusion. Their singles had spent 142 weeks in the top 75 and 99 weeks in the top 40 across 16 UK hits (three making the top ten). The band's albums spent 199 weeks in the top 75,

119 weeks in the top 40 and 31 in the top ten across eight albums. It was a record most bands of the period would be envious of.

'Live' (Cross, Currie, Ure) 4:11

This was a great opening track (later released as a download-only single) for this lineup's return 28 years after *Lament*. 'Live' is bombastic, hits all of Ultravox's signature notes, and has a strong Billy Currie piano through-line. It immediately set fans' minds at rest that, as an album, *Brilliant* was intended as a collection of pure Ultravox songs updated for the 21st century through the use of a combination of new and old technology and new and old approaches to performance and instrumentation. The old magic was clearly intact, if not evenly spread across all the tracks. 'Live' laid down a marker: the old Ultravox was back, and everything old was new again.

Producer Stephen Lipson – who'd worked with Annie Lennox, Frankie Goes to Hollywood, and former Warren Cann collaborator Hans Zimmer – joined the *Brilliant* project at a late stage when most of the songs were already well-developed. There's a strong element of *Quartet*, certainly in the production, with the return of harmonies and backing vocals, strong guitar work with plenty of distortion, excellent construction, and thumping drum work from Warren Cann. Ultravox were back, and this was clearly an Ultravox song, not a beefed-up Midge Ure solo track (an accusation made against some of the album's weaker tracks).

'Live' is also reminiscent of 'Same Old Story' (without the female backing vocals) from the much-disliked *U-Vox*, suggesting that, after their live return, the band may have been rehabilitating some of the stadium-rock approach that song took.

'Flow' (Cross, Currie, Ure) 4:24

Lovely pulsing synth sounds open 'Flow', backed by impressionistic percussion and solid, thudding piano notes. However, the lyric echoes Ure's number one solo hit 'If I Was', planting the suspicion that 'Flow' started as a Ure solo song repurposed for Ultravox.

There's something of U2 about the guitar solo (maybe echoing the work of Robin Guthrie) – a new sound for Ultravox, but the track is saved by Currie's strong synth flourishes. It culminates in a deconstruction to what seems a quieter end (an old Ultravox technique) but then starts up again, only to fade out just as Currie's synths get going again, leaving the listener wanting more. Imagine 'Flow' if it had been given the Conny Plank treatment.

'Brilliant' (Cross, Currie, Ure) 4:22

The first chance fans got to hear the fruits of the reunited band's latest adventures in recording came when the lead single 'Brilliant' was played on BBC Radio 2's Ken Bruce show at 11:36 am on 17 April 2012. It was clearly Ultravox, perhaps not sounding exactly the same as they did in the 1980s but emulating enough of their signature sound to make the identification unmistakable.

The track is driven by a strong 1980s rhythm (wonderfully boosted when played live), bolstered by an excellent piano motif from Currie (as would recur across the album). This was the pure sound of Ultravox. The mid-point instrumental break is brief but welcome, while Ure's whispery vocal (on this and several other tracks on *Brilliant*) is very different from Ultravox in their heyday: used more on the verses than the chorus here. Ure explained the subject of the song: "Brilliant' is a bittersweet comment on pop culture. 'You, the brilliant thing you are/Outshine the brightest star/So distant and too far'. It's about the other side of fame and success, a song about the bright young things that ignore the consequences of fame with the ensuing burnout rate ... In a way, it should read 'Brilliant' with a question mark'.

The cover image did include the hint of a question mark motif in the graphic swirl enclosing the title. This was Ure as a songwriter drawing on his own experience and heritage in show business, which stretched from as far back as the early 1970s. Perhaps fame (and fortune?) was not all it was cracked up to be. On stereoboard.com, Ure put recapturing the signature Ultravox sound down to the personnel involved:

> We've got a very, very weird and strange outlook on music, and this album has Ultravox's DNA running right through it ... That DNA has a lot to do with Billy's classical music upbringing, the way he structures chords and melodies, the way certain notes touch and provoke emotions, and my pop sensibilities and melodies. Once you throw those things together, it's instantly Ultravox ... There's a direct link between what we did 30 years ago and *Brilliant* because it is us. If we'd tried to sit there and emulate what we did 30 years ago, it wouldn't have worked. But luckily for us, if we sit down and do something together, it sounds like Ultravox. We don't try to make it sound like that; it's just what comes out.

'Change' (Cross, Currie, Ure) 4:30

There's a notable change of pace for 'Change', but with the same whispering vocals from Ure and rather plodding and droning synths providing the backing, yet it's a solid 1980s-sounding album track. Currie's synth and piano parts lift things, providing decent context. Overall, this is a consistent track that slightly outstays its welcome. It's also one of several of the album's songs concerned with love, romance and relationships (mainly their aftermath), subjects that were never a big focus for Ultravox. Perhaps greater input from Cann on the lyric side of things would've given a bit more variety (and abstract notions, too). Note the pointed omission of Cann's name from the songwriting credits on *Brilliant* – it seems this was no longer the four-way equitable split of the past. Cann added his drumming separately from the rest of the recording process.

The welcome instrumental break brings Currie's warbling synths to the fore, saving 'Change' from dragging too much, giving the overall feel of a Currie solo-album outtake, crossed with some 'Fade To Grey' synth atmospherics and Ure's whispering vocals layered on top. (Maybe all of the band were searching their cast-offs for material for *Brilliant*.)

'Rise' (Cross, Currie, Ure) 4:04

If you dozed off during 'Change', then the sharp start to 'Rise' would kick you back awake. This is Ultravox tackling up-to-date, 21st-century dance music, playing out over Kraftwerk-style rhythms: a fresh challenge. This is very much a character-narrated song, with Ure almost playing the part of the demon embodied by Oliver Tobias in the 1982 'Hymn' video. It's clear from the chorus what's going on:

Hold on, I've come to help you rise
With a handshake, big smile, good guy profile
Take it now or leave it 'neath the flash of a neon sky
I'll cheat and lie
To give you all the things you need
To help you get the things I need for me

This sounds like a 1980s track attacking yuppiedom or – in a modern context – a song about coercive control, where one party helps the other for selfish ends. There are intriguing lyric callbacks too: 'I give to you the best of everything/I'm here to grow your little monuments' recalls the title of the *Monument* tour, while 'I bring you revelations openly' perhaps inadvertently cites CurrieVox's *Revelation*. The maniacal 'ha ha ha' laughter towards the end is a nice touch, echoing the title of an earlier Ultravox album! Things then end with a very strong, very welcome Currie pitch-bending Giorgio Moroder-influenced synth solo – the kind of thing Currie didn't seem to allow himself on his self-produced 1990s Ultravox albums – building to a definitive end to this distinctly adventurous track.

'Remembering' (Cross, Currie, Ure) 3:43

This slow ballad has the whiff of a repurposed Ure solo track, given extra value from Currie's piano opening. It's a 'Visions In Blue'-style track, in marked contrast to the preceding 'Rise', helped hugely by a nice guitar section – something not always evident on the album (where Cross' bass seems to go missing for entire songs). The segues between these tracks and the hints of New Romantic songs of times past make it interesting, making more of the ominous atmospherics than most of the album's tracks manage to. Some experimental percussion sounds surface occasionally, some violin licks and some synth-driven sound effects – all making for a captivating sonic landscape. The strained Ure vocals are, alas, present and correct, letting things down a little.

'Hello' (Cross, Currie, Ure) 5:40
Everything works together on 'Hello' – guitar, drums, bass (ah, hello!) and piano – resulting in a somewhat gimmicky track that recalls the best of *Quartet*, with a pumping rhythm driven by the piano part, and featuring a stronger thundering vocal from Ure (thank goodness – welcome, despite the heavy processing). There's an epic, widescreen feel to 'Hello' – recalling 'Hymn' – but the lyric's not strong enough to support the dramatic instrumentation.

The album's longest track, 'Hello' has room for more Currie synths late in the game for the final minute or so – welcome – but why is it confined to the end? Where's the soaring central section that used to grace this type of Ultravox track and give Currie's keyboard-playing a good workout? Finally, 'Hello' says 'Goodbye' when it ends with a bang!

'One' (Cross, Currie, Ure) 4:43
The scratchy, experimental opening of 'One' suggests the playing of an old record before this slow ballad bursts into life. Unfortunately, its impact is severely diluted by Ure's feathery vocal and tinny-sounding drums. As on the lead single 'Brilliant' and several other tracks here, the vocal seems weaker than in the past and even in his contemporary live performances. That suggests this approach was a choice for this recording. There's a nice central instrumental section that builds out to a stronger second half, but things peter out on a weak ending. It's a song you'd want to like, but there are so many obstacles – primarily the egregious vocal approach – that 'One' finds itself in the prime position for being the album's worst track. Additionally, just like 'Flow' and 'Remembering', this and the following track 'Fall' sound like potentially repurposed Ure solo efforts worked into Ultravox tracks in name only.

'Fall' (Cross, Currie, Ure) 4:07
Starting with a vocal opening, 'Fall' plays out like another Ure solo track built into something slightly more substantial. Ure's stronger vocals (at the beginning, at least) are nonetheless heavily treated here, while Currie provides a solid synth/piano backing against grinding, crackly rhythms.

Some of the lyric recalls the concerns of several songs on the much-disliked *U-Vox*, with lines like 'Fierce conversations gone on for years' and 'Fighting back words with words of war' suggesting an anti-conflict theme (whether in personal relationships or international relations). The song seems to peter out, only to surprise with a false ending, as it springs back into action with Ure's hefty chorus vocal. The problem is there have been too many similar-sounding tracks in a row, meaning that some of the songs lose their distinction and are not as memorable as they could've been.

'Lie' (Cross, Currie, Ure) 4:35
After several sleepy tracks, 'Lie' is a much-needed injection of pure Ultravox energy, complete with a throbbing, pulsing, driving rhythm, a solid anthemic

vocal from a wide-awake Ure (proving he could do it if he'd wanted to) and a great piano part from Currie, resulting in a sing-along effect, encouraging audiences to join-in during live performances. There's a heavy guitar presence here, a great middle section and a big widescreen sound: all classic Ultravox trademarks. In the past, this could've easily been a hit single. Again, Currie's crunching synths are relegated to seeing the track out.

'Satellite' (Cross, Currie, Ure) 3:58

The drums are to the fore here, with the fast-moving vocal trying to keep up, complete with backing chants, making for a track as strong as anything from the band's past. Finally, just when you thought it couldn't get any better, Currie's much-missed violin is unleashed. Where on Earth has it been for this entire album?

Sounding like a track left on the cutting room floor back in 1980, 'Satellite' reflects the big sound and big production favoured by Ultravox, showcasing this often-bombastic band at their very best. Ure's vocal soars, just like the old days, in fact. It's one of their best tracks since *Rage In Eden*'s 'We Stand Alone', 'The Thin Wall' and 'The Voice'. It exhibits energetic urgency and a compelling rhythm, putting Warren Cann's drumming very much to the fore, as well as those luscious Currie viola licks. This is the very spirit of Ultravox, bottled.

'Contact' (Cross, Currie, Ure) 4:31

Brilliant makes a slow, dignified exit with 'Contact'. It's a bit of a comedown after the driving 'Lie', but Currie's violin playing again stands out. This proved to be a favourite of Ure: 'There are so many equally strong emotions to write about as well as love, which I hope we have used to good effect. My favourite song on the album is the final one: 'Contact'. It reflects how technology has taken over our lives and how we only communicate through that technology. That's modern contact'.

There is something wistful in the lines 'Relive this conversation one last time/Just me in this endless forever/Just me and the sound of a heartbeat, distant drum'. Nonetheless, 'Contact' was an underwhelming close to a much-anticipated album.

At least *Brilliant* exists, whatever its faults, as, without it, the Cann-less 'pink thing' *U-Vox* would stand as the final Ultravox album. It's much better they went out on a *Brilliant* note, after all.

Related Tracks
'7/8' (Cross, Currie, Ure) 4:28
A B-side or extra track along with the 'Live' single download, '7/8' is a pleasant enough, melodic piano-driven effort that hints at drama but never quite achieves it. It's a bit airy and a bit spacey, with vocal hints throughout and electronic percussion backing. That said, it would've been a strong closer for *Brilliant*, bringing things full circle from the *Vienna* opener 'Astradyne'.

Bibliography

Charlesworth, C., *Ultravox: In Their Own Words* (Omnibus Press, 1984)
Evans, R., *Listening To The Sounds The Machines Make* (Omnibus Press, 2022)
Jones, D., *Sweet Dreams: From Club Culture To Style Culture* (Faber & Faber, 2020)
Smith, G., *We Can Be Heroes: London Clubland 1976-1984* (Unbound, 2011)
Ure, M., *If I Was* (Virgin Books, 2004)

Additional works
Issue of *Sounds, Record Mirror, NME, Melody Maker, ZigZag, Smash Hits, New Styles New Sounds, Blitz, The Face, Q Electro-Pop Special Edition* (2005)
Electronic Sound #69 (2020)
Classic Pop SynthPop Special Edition Volume II: Electric Dreams (2020)
In The City fanzine (Editors: Francis Drake, Peter Gilbert)
The Past, Present, And Future Of Ultravox (Editors: Francis Drake, Peter Gilbert)
Ultravox Information Service (UIS, Editors: Francis Drake, Peter Gilbert)
Extreme Voice fanzine (#1-20, Editors: Cerise A. Reed, Robin Harris)
re:VOX fanzine (#1-21, Editor: Rob Kirby)

Websites
Especially useful were threads and pages at *punk77.co.uk, ultravox.hpage.com, ultravox.org.uk, forums.stevehoffman.tv, postpunkmonk.com* and Jonas Warstad's online interview with Warren Cann.

Also consulted: *Wikipedia, wearecult.rocks, recordcollectormag.com, classicpopmag.com, udiscovermusic.com, musicianguide.com, audio-advent.ghost.io, rockandrollglobe.com, thevogue.com, electricityclub.co.uk, golden80s.com, nostalgiacentral.com, pleasekillme.com, theguardian.com, theaudiophileman.com, popmatters.com, quietcity.co.uk, scotsman.com, independent.co.uk, midgeure.co.uk, soundonsound.com, moredarkthanshark.org, rockremnants.com, discog.info, trouserpress.com, officialcharts.com, youtube.com*

Depeche Mode - *on track*
every album, every song

Brian J. Robb
Paperback
176 pages
41 colour photographs
978-1-78952-277-8
£15.99
$22.95

**Every album and
every song by this
world-renowned
electronic rock band.**

For four decades, Depeche Mode dominated electronic music, from the naïve melodies of 1981's *Speak & Spell* through to 2023's *Memento Mori*. Through changing line-ups featuring Vince Clarke, Alan Wilder, and Andy Fletcher, singer Dave Gahan and main songwriter Martin Gore have been the band's core. Starting as teenagers and now in their 60s, they have survived worldwide fame, addictions to drink and drugs, and near-death experiences, while continuing to innovate as technology and the music business evolved.

An acclaimed live band, it is through their fifteen studio albums that Depeche Mode have best expressed themselves,

from the industrial darkness of *Black Celebration* (1986) to their popular breakthroughs with *Music For the Masses* (1987) and *Violator* (1990) and the emotional upheaval of 1993's *Songs of Faith and Devotion*.

The band survived the chaotic fallout from that album and tour in the mid-1990s, with Gahan experiencing a near-fatal drug overdose, to regroup with *Ultra* (1997). They continued their explorations of love, death, sex, and politics on acclaimed albums *Playing the Angel* (2005), *Delta Machine* (2013), and *Spirit* (2016). Inducted into the Rock and Roll Hall of Fame in 2020, proven survivors Depeche Mode have their story told here in song-by-song detail.

The Human League And The Sheffield Electro Scene
- *on track* every album, every song

Andrew Darlington
Paperback
176 pages
47 colour photographs
978-1-78952-186-3
£15.99
$22.95

Every album and every song by this hugely successful pop/electronica band and the bands that emerged at the same time.

Sheffield, in the late-1970s, was isolated from what was happening in London in the same way that Liverpool had been in 1963. A unique generation of electro-experimental groupings evolved in the former Steel City around Cabaret Voltaire and The Future. The Future split into two factions, Clock DVA and The Human League, the latter splitting into two further factions - Heaven 17 and The Human League as we now know them, fronted by Philip Oakey with Joanne Catherall and Susan Sulley.

Dare became one of the most iconic albums of the eighties; the album by which The Human League are most instantly recognised. It is an ambitious record, both driven and voracious, with giddy grenades of inventiveness. A triumph of content over style, at once phenomenally commercial and gleefully avant-garde.

The American success of 'Don't You Want Me', accelerated by the high-gloss video, which exploited the band's visual appeal, heralded what was soon termed the 'second British invasion'. It was the first of two singles by the band to top US charts.

This book tells the full story, from the scene's origins in Sheffield through the full arc of the very early Heaven 17 albums and the complete Human League discography into the twenty-first century.

On Track Series

AC/DC – Chris Sutton 978-1-78952-307-2

Allman Brothers Band – Andrew Wild 978-1-78952-252-5

Tori Amos – Lisa Torem 978-1-78952-142-9

Aphex Twin – Beau Waddell 978-1-78952-267-9

Asia – Peter Braidis 978-1-78952-099-6

Badfinger – Robert Day-Webb 978-1-878952-176-4

Barclay James Harvest – Keith and Monica Domone 978-1-78952-067-5

Beck – Arthur Lizie 978-1-78952-258-7

The Beat, General Public, Fine Young Cannibals – Steve Parry 978-1-78952-274-7

The Beatles – Andrew Wild 978-1-78952-009-5

The Beatles Solo 1969-1980 – Andrew Wild 978-1-78952-030-9

Blue Oyster Cult – Jacob Holm-Lupo 978-1-78952-007-1

Blur – Matt Bishop 978-178952-164-1

Marc Bolan and T.Rex – Peter Gallagher 978-1-78952-124-5

Kate Bush – Bill Thomas 978-1-78952-097-2

The Byrds – Andy McArthur 978-1-78952-280-8

Camel – Hamish Kuzminski 978-1-78952-040-8

Captain Beefheart – Opher Goodwin 978-1-78952-235-8

Caravan – Andy Boot 978-1-78952-127-6

Cardiacs – Eric Benac 978-1-78952-131-3

Wendy Carlos – Mark Marrington 978-1-78952-331-7

The Carpenters – Paul Tornbohm 978-1-78952-301-0

Nick Cave and The Bad Seeds – Dominic Sanderson 978-1-78952-240-2

Eric Clapton Solo – Andrew Wild 978-1-78952-141-2

The Clash – Nick Assirati 978-1-78952-077-4

Elvis Costello and The Attractions – Georg Purvis 978-1-78952-129-0

Crosby, Stills and Nash – Andrew Wild 978-1-78952-039-2

Creedence Clearwater Revival – Tony Thompson 978-178952-237-2

The Damned – Morgan Brown 978-1-78952-136-8

David Bowie 1964 to 1982 – Carl Ewens 978-1-78952-324-9

Deep Purple and Rainbow 1968-79 – Steve Pilkington 978-1-78952-002-6

Depeche Mode – Brian J. Robb 978-1-78952-277-8

Dire Straits – Andrew Wild 978-1-78952-044-6

The Divine Comedy – Alan Draper 978-1-78952-308-9

The Doors – Tony Thompson 978-1-78952-137-5

Dream Theater – Jordan Blum 978-1-78952-050-7

Bob Dylan 1962-1970 – Opher Goodwin 978-1-78952-275-2

Eagles – John Van der Kiste 978-1-78952-260-0

Earth, Wind and Fire – Bud Wilkins 978-1-78952-272-3

Electric Light Orchestra – Barry Delve 978-1-78952-152-8

Nektar – Scott Meze – 978-1-78952-257-0
New Order – Dennis Remmer – 978-1-78952-249-5
Nightwish – Simon McMurdo – 978-1-78952-270-9
Nirvana – William E. Spevack 978-1-78952-318-8
Laura Nyro – Philip Ward 978-1-78952-182-5
Oasis – 978-1-78952-300-3
Mike Oldfield – Ryan Yard 978-1-78952-060-6
Opeth – Jordan Blum 978-1-78-952-166-5
Pearl Jam – Ben L. Connor 978-1-78952-188-7
Tom Petty – Richard James 978-1-78952-128-3
Pink Floyd – Richard Butterworth 978-1-78952-242-6
The Police – Pete Braidis 978-1-78952-158-0
Porcupine Tree – Nick Holmes 978-1-78952-144-3
Procol Harum – Scott Meze 978-1-78952-315-7
Queen – Andrew Wild 978-1-78952-003-3
Radiohead – William Allen 978-1-78952-149-8
Rancid – Paul Matts 978-1-78952-187-0
Lou Reed 1972-1986 – Ethan Roy 978-1-78952-283-9
Renaissance – David Detmer 978-1-78952-062-0
REO Speedwagon – Jim Romag 978-1-78952-262-4
The Rolling Stones 1963-80 – Steve Pilkington 978-1-78952-017-0
Linda Ronstadt 1969-1989 – Daryl O. Lawrence
Sensational Alex Harvey Band – Peter Gallagher 978-1-7952-289-1
The Small Faces and The Faces – Andrew Darlington 978-1-78952-316-4
The Smashing Pumpkins – Matt Karpe 978-1-7952-291-4
The Smiths and Morrissey – Tommy Gunnarsson 978-1-78952-140-5
Spirit – Rev. Keith A. Gordon – 978-1-78952- 248-8
Soft Machine – Scott Meze 978-1078952-271-6
Stackridge – Alan Draper 978-1-78952-232-7
Status Quo the Frantic Four Years – Richard James 978-1-78952-160-3
Steely Dan – Jez Rowden 978-1-78952-043-9
The Stranglers – Martin Hutchinson 978-1-78952-323-2
Talk Talk – Gary Steel 978-1-78952-284-6
Tears For Fears – Paul Clark – 978-178952-238-9
Thin Lizzy – Graeme Stroud 978-1-78952-064-4
Tool – Matt Karpe 978-1-78952-234-1
Toto – Jacob Holm-Lupo 978-1-78952-019-4
U2 – Eoghan Lyng 978-1-78952-078-1
UFO – Richard James 978-1-78952-073-6
Ultravox – Brian J. Robb 978-1-78952-330-0
Van Der Graaf Generator – Dan Coffey 978-1-78952-031-6
Van Halen – Morgan Brown – 9781-78952-256-3

Suzanne Vega – Lisa Torem 978-1-78952-281-5
Jack White And The White Stripes – Ben L. Connor 978-1-78952-303-4
The Who – Geoffrey Feakes 978-1-78952-076-7
Roy Wood and the Move – James R Turner 978-1-78952-008-8
Yes (new edition) – Stephen Lambe 978-1-78952-282-2
Neil Young 1963 to 1970 – Oper Goodwin 978-1-78952-298-3
Frank Zappa 1966 to 1979 – Eric Benac 978-1-78952-033-0
Warren Zevon – Peter Gallagher 978-1-78952-170-2
The Zombies – Emma Stott 978-1-78952-297-6
10CC – Peter Kearns 978-1-78952-054-5

Decades Series

The Bee Gees in the 1960s – Andrew Mon Hughes et al 978-1-78952-148-1
The Bee Gees in the 1970s – Andrew Mon Hughes et al 978-1-78952-179-5
Black Sabbath in the 1970s – Chris Sutton 978-1-78952-171-9
Britpop – Peter Richard Adams and Matt Pooler 978-1-78952-169-6
Phil Collins in the 1980s – Andrew Wild 978-1-78952-185-6
Alice Cooper in the 1970s – Chris Sutton 978-1-78952-104-7
Alice Cooper in the 1980s – Chris Sutton 978-1-78952-259-4
Curved Air in the 1970s – Laura Shenton 978-1-78952-069-9
Donovan in the 1960s – Jeff Fitzgerald 978-1-78952-233-4
Bob Dylan in the 1980s – Don Klees 978-1-78952-157-3
Brian Eno in the 1970s – Gary Parsons 978-1-78952-239-6
Faith No More in the 1990s – Matt Karpe 978-1-78952-250-1
Fleetwood Mac in the 1970s – Andrew Wild 978-1-78952-105-4
Fleetwood Mac in the 1980s – Don Klees 978-178952-254-9
Focus in the 1970s – Stephen Lambe 978-1-78952-079-8
Free and Bad Company in the 1970s – John Van der Kiste 978-1-78952-178-8
Genesis in the 1970s – Bill Thomas 978178952-146-7
George Harrison in the 1970s – Eoghan Lyng 978-1-78952-174-0
Kiss in the 1970s – Peter Gallagher 978-1-78952-246-4
Manfred Mann's Earth Band in the 1970s – John Van der Kiste 978178952-243-3
Marillion in the 1980s – Nathaniel Webb 978-1-78952-065-1
Van Morrison in the 1970s – Peter Childs – 978-1-78952-241-9
Mott the Hoople & Ian Hunter in the 1970s – John Van der Kiste 978-1-78-952-162-7
Pink Floyd In The 1970s – Georg Purvis 978-1-78952-072-9
Suzi Quatro in the 1970s – Darren Johnson 978-1-78952-236-5
Queen in the 1970s – James Griffiths 978-1-78952-265-5
Roxy Music in the 1970s – Dave Thompson 978-1-78952-180-1
Slade in the 1970s – Darren Johnson 978-1-78952-268-6
Status Quo in the 1980s – Greg Harper 978-1-78952-244-0

Tangerine Dream in the 1970s – Stephen Palmer 978-1-78952-161-0
The Sweet in the 1970s – Darren Johnson 978-1-78952-139-9
Uriah Heep in the 1970s – Steve Pilkington 978-1-78952-103-0
Van der Graaf Generator in the 1970s – Steve Pilkington 978-1-78952-245-7
Rick Wakeman in the 1970s – Geoffrey Feakes 978-1-78952-264-8
Yes in the 1980s – Stephen Lambe with David Watkinson 978-1-78952-125-2

Rock Classics Series
90125 by Yes – Stephen Lambe 978-1-78952-329-4
Bat Out Of Hell by Meatloaf – Geoffrey Feakes 978-1-78952-320-1
Bringing It All Back Home by Bob Dylan – Opher Goodwin 978-1-78952-314-0
Crime Of The Century by Supertramp – Steve Pilkington 978-1-78952-327-0
Let It Bleed by The Rolling Stones – John Van der Kiste 978-1-78952-309-6
Purple Rain by Prince – Matt Karpe 978-1-78952-322-5

On Screen Series
Carry On... – Stephen Lambe 978-1-78952-004-0
David Cronenberg – Patrick Chapman 978-1-78952-071-2
Doctor Who: The David Tennant Years – Jamie Hailstone 978-1-78952-066-8
James Bond – Andrew Wild 978-1-78952-010-1
Monty Python – Steve Pilkington 978-1-78952-047-7
Seinfeld Seasons 1 to 5 – Stephen Lambe 978-1-78952-012-5

Other Books
1967: A Year In Psychedelic Rock 978-1-78952-155-9
1970: A Year In Rock – John Van der Kiste 978-1-78952-147-4
1972: The Year Progressive Rock Ruled The World – Kevan Furbank 978-1-78952-288-4
1973: The Golden Year of Progressive Rock 978-1-78952-165-8
Babysitting A Band On The Rocks – G.D. Praetorius 978-1-78952-106-1
Eric Clapton Sessions – Andrew Wild 978-1-78952-177-1
Dark Horse Records – Aaron Badgley 978-1-78952-287-7
Derek Taylor: For Your Radioactive Children – Andrew Darlington 978-1-78952-038-5
The Golden Age of Easy Listening – Derek Taylor 978-1-78952-285-3
The Golden Road: The Recording History of The Grateful Dead –
John Kilbride 978-1-78952-156-6
His Love – Andrew Wild 978-1-78952-278-5
Iggy and The Stooges On Stage 1967-1974 – Per Nilsen 978-1-78952-101-6
Jon Anderson and the Warriors – the road to Yes – David Watkinson 978-1-78952-059-0
Magic: The David Paton Story – David Paton 978-1-78952-266-2
Misty: The Music of Johnny Mathis – Jakob Baekgaard 978-1-78952-247-1
Nu Metal: A Definitive Guide – Matt Karpe 978-1-78952-063-7

Remembering Live Aid – Andrew Wild 978-1-78952-328-7
Tommy Bolin: In and Out of Deep Purple – Laura Shenton 978-1-78952-070-5
Maximum Darkness – Deke Leonard 978-1-78952-048-4
The Twang Dynasty – Deke Leonard 978-1-78952-049-1

And Many More To Come!

Would you like to write for Sonicbond Publishing?

At Sonicbond Publishing we are always on the look-out for authors, particularly for our two main series:

On Track. Mixing fact with in depth analysis, the On Track series examines the work of a particular musical artist or group. All genres are considered from easy listening and jazz to 60s soul to 90s pop, via rock and metal.

On Screen. This series looks at the world of film and television. Subjects considered include directors, actors and writers, as well as entire television and film series. As with the On Track series, we balance fact with analysis.

While professional writing experience would, of course, be an advantage the most important qualification is to have real enthusiasm and knowledge of your subject. First-time authors are welcomed, but the ability to write well in English is essential.

Sonicbond Publishing has distribution throughout Europe and North America, and all books are also published in E-book form. Authors will be paid a royalty based on sales of their book.

Further details are available from www.sonicbondpublishing.co.uk. To contact us, complete the contact form there or
email info@sonicbondpublishing.co.uk